September 11th
And Beyond

September 11th
And Beyond

20 Parables for our time

Paul Johns

John Hunt
Publishing Limited

Contents

Dedication

These stories are dedicated to Martin, Naomi and Neil.

Introduction

I wrote these stories because I enjoy writing stories. They are fiction, products of my imagination, such as it is.

But the fiction is anchored. The stories are all set in the world as we are discovering it since September 11th 2001. Each one refers more or less directly to events reported in newspapers, or seen on TV.

The stories also use material which you'll find in the Bible – events, sayings, poetry, and stories older and better than mine. I find the Bible full of imaginative insights which throw light on today's events; just as today's events illuminate the Bible.*

It's never easy to make sense of the big unfolding issues of our time, while we're living through them. It's been a particular struggle for me since September 11th. I've felt the world shifting under my feet. But I've discovered that if I let my imagination out to play – and stories are a good way of doing that – I can sometimes catch sight of something deeper going on beneath the surface of the news.

I hope it doesn't sound pretentious to call these stories parables. I use the word simply to indicate that I hope they serve as windows shedding a little light on events more important than the stories themselves, events which have darkened the world since September 11th.

I certainly don't claim that these stories reveal Truth with a capital T. I happen to believe that truth is something you should never claim to know without doubt; but something you should always keep trying to discover. And, I think, you need imagination to discover truth.

Attempting these stories has set my imagination going. Perhaps reading or telling them will set yours going too.

Paul Johns
June 2002

*There is a list of the Bible references on page 119.

God bless America

In the days immediately after September 11th there was
widespread sympathy for the American people. But in the
media on both sides of the Atlantic there were also
comments to the effect that America's suffering was not
unique; that people in other countries live with war and
terror every day; and that America, by its policies and
values, had perhaps brought its suffering upon itself. Mayor
Giuliani of New York dismissed talk of 'moral relativities...
We are right and they (terrorists) are wrong; it's as simple
as that.' And President Bush described the USA as
'the most free nation in the world'.

The sun was setting. It was a glorious summer's evening in heaven.
God was sitting on the verandah, enjoying the beauty of the garden, the
scent of honeysuckle on the trellis, bright flowers bordering the lawn
which stretched down to the woods, and beyond the woods the
mountains, their varied colours sharp in the setting sun.

The garden gate clicked. God looked up. There was Satan.

'God bless America,' said Satan, packing a great deal of subtle
menace into three words.

America was of course the richest, most powerful nation on earth.
She was secure, safe from any other nation. She was also the land of the
free. Many people, oppressed in their own homelands, had found
freedom within her borders.

God often thought about America. 'She may not see freedom quite as
I see it', he reflected, 'She's inclined to confuse it with wealth and
power; but at least she's looking in the right direction.' God liked that.
He liked to feel that America shared something of his own vision,
though through a glass darkly. For setting people free was God's

business; 'especially', he thought as he looked at his unwelcome visitor, 'setting them free from this creature'.

'God bless America,' Satan repeated.

'What do you want?'

'You know why America loves you?' asked Satan.

'Go on,' said God. He had a nasty feeling that Satan was reading his thoughts.

'You think America loves you because America loves freedom? Well you're wrong. America loves you because she loves her wealth and power. Want me to prove it to you? Let me knock down her high tower, spread a little pain around her city. Then see what happens. Then see whether she says, "God bless America"'.

'No' said God, firmly. 'No!'

But even as he said it, God knew that his 'no' was ambiguous.

'Ah!' said Satan, quickly reading God's mind again. 'Do you mean "No, you mustn't damage America"? Or do you mean "No, because I'm afraid Satan might be right"? Think carefully. Let me know.'

And with that Satan disappeared. He would return. He always did.

For a long while, God walked up and down the garden deep in thought. The shadows were lengthening on the lawn. Slowly the setting sun deserted the distant hills, dissolving their colours into a dull grey, and the evening air grew cool. God sensed an impending crisis in heaven.

'I love America for her love of freedom,' said God to himself. 'But suppose America loves me only for her privileges.'

God, like people he'd created the world over, wanted to be loved, for love's sake. That's why he wanted them to be free.

'But suppose Satan's right', thought God. 'Suppose America values wealth and power more than freedom. Suppose she is not, after all, my kindred spirit on earth. Suppose she is using me to endorse her privileges. Then "God bless America" is counterfeit; and I am another American idol, another tall tower. And what about the other nations? Have I become everywhere just a projection of human self-interest pointing upwards? Is the world using my name as Satan does?'

Satan was probing the paradox at the heart of heaven. God felt the pain of it. 'You must be free before you can love selflessly. But only selfless love can set you free. If I set limits to freedom, even Satan's, I set limits to love, even mine.'

God knew he could not refuse the challenge. Yet the risks were terrible. 'Suppose I allow Satan to attack America, what then – more suffering, anger, fear, hatred, political tension breaking out all round the world; forbearance, wisdom, vision tested to destruction? Every day people pray to me, "Do not lead us to the time of trial,"' thought God. 'Yet that's exactly what I am going to do. And then people will say there is no God who cares!' God broke out in a cold sweat.

And now it was night in heaven's garden. The garden gate clicked. God sensed movement along the darkened lawn. Satan had come back for an answer.

One morning, months later, a plane descended out of a cloudless sky. The pilot could see clearly the airstrip at the other end of the isolated valley in the mountains. He could see further. Beyond the airstrip the mountains joined and closed the valley. And there, built into the hillside, was the great smooth curve of a multi-storey building, its long vertical windows touched with gold by the early sun. It looked like a grand entrance into the depths of the earth.

The pilot landed the plane smoothly in the still, morning air. He taxied to a halt a short distance from the low rectangular airport building and noted the armed guards positioned around the entrance and on the roof. He watched as a black saloon car left the building and approached his plane. The driver opened the rear door of the car. A uniformed official opened the door of the plane, descended the steps, turned, and waited as the sole passenger emerged – a tall elegant woman. She was dressed wholly in black.

She got into the car. The car quickly covered the short distance to the airport building. There was a brief pause for formalities. A few minutes later the black saloon was climbing the winding road to the great building on the mountainside.

At the grand portico entrance to the building, the President of the World Institute for Moral Science was about to receive a very important visitor – America.

He descended the steps, with his two most senior colleagues, to greet her as she stepped out of the car.

'Welcome to the Institute, madam,' he said. 'I am, as you know, Dr Eliphaz. These are my colleagues, Dr Bildad and Dr Zophar.' They shook hands in turn.

'You are most welcome, madam. And you have our deepest condolences.'

'Thank you,' said woman with a wan smile. 'But you know why I have come – not for condolences, but for answers. I need to know. You understand that?'

'We understand. Our mission is to research and provide answers. Here on this mountainside,' he gestured at the frontage of the building, 'we are well placed to mine for answers in the depths of the earth, distanced from the passions which… er…so often cloud human understanding, especially, if I may say so, in times of crisis. It is our privilege to help you,' said Dr. Eliphaz. 'Please come inside.'

The President of the Institute and his senior colleagues showed America round the laboratories. They took her a little way into the great mineshaft, which they had hollowed out of the mountain at the back of the building. They entertained her to a lavish lunch. Then they led her to the conference room. The afternoon sun, high over the mountains, was streaming through the long vertical widow. As she sat, America noticed the clouds now gathering around the mountaintop.

'So you see, madam,' said Dr Eliphaz, summing up, 'Dr Bildad here, through his study of the structure of this mountain range, has obtained a… er, I may say… a unique understanding of the mechanics of morality.' He pointed to a series of triangular images on a screen on the wall. 'There is, as you can see, a… a moral mechanism at work in the world. Each nation has its own pendulum, so to speak, each person too. Each good deed moves the pendulum one way and… er… each bad deed moves it the other. At the pivot of the pendulum… er … we are not yet sure exactly how this operates… there is some kind of valve, which releases pain and pleasure into the world according to the swing of the pendulum. And thus we think… er… we are confident… that the distribution of good and bad fortune is determined by the interaction of millions of valves, of pendulums. The concept is beautiful in its simplicity, but its operation is… is immensely delicate and complex.'

Dr Eliphaz paused. America looked at the screen but said nothing.

'And.' Dr Eliphaz went on, 'Dr Zophar's analysis of the many seams of suffering solidified in the mountain range has brought him very close to an understanding of the correlation being different categories of wrongdoing and different kinds and degrees of suffering.'

'So are you telling me that my suffering… ?' began America

'Er… yes' said Dr Eliphaz. 'I know this must be painful for you at a time of such distress. And, believe me, we are trying to help you. But we are convinced that since the consequence of wrongdoing is some form of suffering… er… as I say, the correlation is not yet fully understood, so we cannot be precise… therefore, if you are suffering, you must have done… no, let me put it this way, there must have been some wrongdoing… with which you have been associated, to… to… to justify, or perhaps I should say to explain, the suffering.'

As Dr Eliphaz unfolded this answer, America fixed her eyes steadily on him. When he had finished, she got up and walked to the window. She looked at the clouded mountain, the apparent source of all this moral wisdom. The men looked at her back, sympathetic toward their distinguished guest, but satisfied with their conclusions.

America turned and faced them. Her eyes met theirs. She spoke to Dr Eliphaz.

'No,' said America. 'No, Dr Eliphaz. I thank you for your explanation. But I cannot accept it.'

'But madam… ' said Dr Bildad, 'the evidence is… ' Dr Eliphaz gestured to him to be silent.

'I can't accept what you tell me,' America repeated. 'I don't deny that I may have done wrong. Nations are human. Every nation goes astray in policy sometimes. But I know I have done right too. Have I not been a champion of freedom?'

'The moral mechanism allows for that,' said Dr Zophar. 'The pivotal system… '

America brushed him aside. 'But what have you to say about pure evil, evil without cause, the evil that destroyed my tower, and all the people in it! And what have you got to say about pure spontaneous goodness, the goodness of my fire fighters? Dr Zophar, when you went mining in that mountain,' she pointed out of the window, 'did you tunnel into the seams of unmerited suffering, suffering of innocent women and children? Because there's a great deal of that buried in the upheavals of the world over the centuries; a great deal still to be buried.'

'Well,' said Dr Zophar, 'my research into suffering is of course ongoing, but I… '

'I may be governed less by head, more by heart than you all are,' said America, bypassing him with mounting emotion. 'But I can't accept that the collapse of my tower, and all my suffering, is all due to your moral mechanics. You'll be telling me that it was the will of God next!'

'Ah!' said Dr Eliphas, as though he had just found the missing final piece of a jigsaw. 'I was going to bring God into this. You see, we believe… that is er… Dr Bildad's research suggests that God is… as it were, behind the moral mechanism… the pivot of the pendulum.'

'If you are telling me,' America was passionate now, 'that God caused this suffering – the destruction of the tower, the torrent of distress on city streets, and now the plague of fear across the nation… if that's the work of your god, then all I ask is that your god leaves me alone. I would rather no moral order, no god than a punitive one. Dr Eliphaz, I do not intend to worship a… a pendulum!'

She turned to face the window. The sun shone no longer. Dark storm clouds were gathering over the mountain. Rain trickled down the long window.

'Madam,' said Dr Eliphaz, gently speaking to her back, 'your reaction is understandable, indeed predictable. We know from Dr Zophar's work on elemental suffering that… '

'Never mind your work!' cried America, turning on him, and near to tears. 'I know that I am suffering. And I know that I do not deserve this suffering. And I know that I am going to punish the one who caused it.'

'Then, madam,' said Dr Eliphaz coolly, 'you are operating within the moral mechanism the very existence of which you seem to deny.' He switched off the display on the screen.

'I think I had better go,' said America. 'Please call the car.'

The three academics stood up. Dr Eliphaz pressed his desk button to summon the chauffer. 'Madam,' he said, speaking like a doctor to a patient who has just refused life-saving treatment, 'I am sorry if our… er… attempt to help you falls short of your expectations. You must of course do as you wish. But thank you for visiting us. And I repeat, our condolences to you and your loved ones.'

Outside it was now very dark and raining heavily. A thunderstorm enveloped the mountain above the Institute.

America spoke to the chauffer. 'Up the hill!' she said.

'Up, madam? But… '

'Yes, up – as far as you can safely drive. Then I will walk.'

'But, madam… '

'Please do as I ask.'

A quarter of an hour later, the chauffer sat and watched as America, her cloak wrapped round her against the storm, advanced up the rough track. Soon, with the rain driving against the windscreen, he could see her no more.

America climbed and climbed the rocky path, the storm beating down on her. She was well above the Institute now. Exhausted, she found a fissure in the mountain face, a cave, for shelter. Outside stood a small leafless tree, a trunk with few broken branches. She went into the cave, leaned against the wall and stood very still, her heart beating fast.

'My dear, you have no idea how glad I am to see you,' said God speaking clearly out of the storm. 'And I am sorry, so very sorry.'

The words were like a warm embrace. America cried.

'But why?' she asked. 'Why? I cannot accept the word of the Institute.'

'You are right not to,' said God. 'I know their work. I just wish they would spend a little less time burrowing inside the mountain, and a little more up here on top of it. You are right, my dear, I am not the pivot of a pendulum. I do not operate through valves.'

America could feel God smiling at her.

'But why?' she asked again, through tears. 'People ask "Why America?" Why the suffering of the good and innocent?'

'Those are two separate questions,' said God.

'You mean I am guilty and deserve the suffering?'

'I didn't say that, though I think you have been guilty of believing in an illusion – the illusion that you were somehow special, destined to be uniquely secure, that you could build towers without risk. And you know that's not true now. Fortunate you may be in many ways; but you are bound in the same bundle as the rest of the living, with all the trouble that freedom can bring.'

'So you have given me a nasty shock? Suffering is your corrective punishment for the proud?'

'No, I didn't say that?'

'What then?'

'Listen carefully,' said God. 'You ask why innocent suffering. I cannot answer your question in the sense in which you ask it – not now. But in another sense – a very important one – you have already answered it yourself.'

'How?'

'You have discovered the truth that the Institute missed. Our meeting point is not Dr Bildad's pivot. It is your suffering. I heard you cry. In your pain we met. I am in your suffering. I share it. And through suffering I redeem suffering.'

A great sheet of lightning suddenly silhouetted the bare tree outside the cave.

'Look after freedom for me!' thundered God from beyond the tree.

'God bless America,' said America.

A while later, Dr Eliphaz watched from the long window as the aircraft took off into a clearing sky. 'I'm afraid we may have seen the last of a generous benefactor,' he thought to himself.

Meanwhile God had gone back to heaven to do some gardening.

A letter to
the President

On September 15th 2001, two parents, whose son was
killed in the World Trade Centre, sent to the New
York Times an open letter, addressed to President
Bush. In the tense days immediately following
September 11th, Americans were warned by the White
House Press Secretary to 'watch what they say,
watch what they do'.

The king stood, looking out of his window. He watched the strong
wind, tearing the autumn leaves from the trees, driving them in
disorder across the grass, under a gloomy sky. He thought of his
people, many already fleeing the battle to come. 'You don't choose to
go into a war without a good chance of winning,' he thought. His little
country was not strong; his allies were uncertain. But to surrender to
this great pagan army was unthinkable. Any voice suggesting
otherwise must be silenced.

The wind rose. The king moved to the fireside, sat down, and from
the table beside him, he picked up a document, and began to read. He
already knew what it said. The words made him angry. He got to the
end of the first page, folded it, tore it and threw it on the fire. He read
half of the second page, then destroyed that. He didn't bother to read
the remaining pages. One by one, with deliberate anger, he tore each
sheet; and when he had torn them all, he threw them on the fire also.
'A lone voice,' he said, 'can always be silenced.'

Far away and centuries later a great crowd has gathered in a great hall
in great darkness. Goodness knows how many there are, hundreds,

perhaps thousands, sitting row upon unseen row, radiating back, concentric circle upon circle. The hall is filled with subdued murmur.

In the centre is a single spotlight. It shines on a table, and around the table are three empty chairs. All has been deliberately arranged.

By the light of the spot, you can just discern the faces of the people sitting on the front row. There's an old woman with wrinkled face and bright eyes. You notice her, because of her eyes, and because she's wearing a royal blue headscarf, its sheen bright in the light.

Then, from the dark, a couple enter the light. Both are middle aged and well dressed. The man has his arm round the woman. Glance at her face, and you can see her eyes sparkling with the residue of tears. The man guides his wife to the table, to a chair, then sits next to her. The murmuring ceases; and the dark hall falls silent.

The man and woman both turn to look up at the figure who has followed them in – a shabby old man, tall but stooping a little, in a crumpled suit. He sits on the third chair, opposite them.

The husband has a document in his hand and he pushes it across the table to the old man. The old man reads it. The silence is intense now.

'So this is the letter?' he asks. His voice is more resonant, more powerful than you might expect from so old, so apparently frail a figure.

'What do you think?' asks the woman drying her eyes.

The old man looks at her gently.

'So you're going to send this letter to the President?'

'That's right,' said the man, 'for the sake of our son.'

'And others' says his wife. She takes her husband's hand and he smiles at her correction.

'Right' says the old man. 'Let's go through it.'

He runs his finger down the page, as he quotes from their letter.

' "Our son is among the many missing from the World Trade Centre attack. We have shared grief, flickering hope, then despair with his wife…" Good!' says the old man. 'But may I make a suggestion?' he asks gently.

'Please,' says the husband.

'Well this disaster is communal isn't it? The planes hit the two towers; thousands have died; the suffering has darkened the whole city. I think you can be more graphic. So why not add "Death has come in through our windows, cutting off the children from the streets, and the young men from the squares. We looked for peace; but there came terror"?

'That's rather dramatic, rather… biblical, isn't it?' asks the husband.

The old man smiles. 'I'm sorry; it's just my way of seeing things. You must decide. It's your letter.' He pauses, distracted by the movement of chairs somewhere in the darkness of the hall. Then he continues. 'Here's another point. You say: "… we sense that our government is heading in the direction of violent revenge, with the prospect of innocent people dying in distant lands…" '

The old man pauses again, and looks out into the hall, for there is more movement of chairs in the dark. Someone is evidently trying to come to the front. The old woman in the royal blue headscarf stands up, moves to one side to make way for a much younger woman carrying a baby, walking weakly towards the table, towards the light.

The old man stands immediately and helps her into his chair. She slumps, exhausted.

'You have come a long way?' he asks, though he knows the answer.

The young woman says nothing; she simply stares at the couple, with wide eyes. The hall has fallen silent again.

'From Afghanistan, I guess,' says the husband kindly.

His wife turns to the old man. 'Our letter is for her sake too,' she says.

'There's a great evil going from nation to nation,' says the old man, standing now, and with a raised voice half addressing the people in the darkness, 'a great tempest stirring.'

The husband and wife are not quite sure what he means. Does he mean terrorism, with more to come, or does he mean their nations' response to terrorism, or both?

'Jeremiah,' says the husband, 'You don't mind if I call you that?'

'It's my name' says the old man. 'I'm sorry. Let's get back to the letter. "Your response to this attack makes us feel that our government is using our son's memory as a justification to cause suffering to other sons and parents in other lands." Well,' says Jeremiah, 'I suppose the answer to that will be that justice demands the punishment of the terrorists. But then you have to ask: "Should justice be dealt to the terrorists at the expense of injustice to… " (he gently touches the hand of the Afghan woman) "to… to this poor woman?" '

And, turning his back on the table, addressing his unseen audience, he goes on: 'Justice is not something to be invoked when it suits you. Justice, justice with compassion, is God's consistent persistent demand. Let rulers remember this.'

The wife touches his arm, with a smile. 'Jeremiah, we haven't much time. The letter?'

'O yes, forgive me,' says Jeremiah, and, still standing, he reads on. ' "We urge you" (that's the President?) "to think about how to develop peaceful and rational solutions to terrorism, solutions that do not sink us to the inhuman level of terrorists. Sincerely yours." Excellent! Excellent!'

And turning again to his global audience he goes on in a voice the power of which surprises the man and his wife, and which makes the Afghan woman raise her tired, scarcely comprehending eyes to his face.

'Hear this letter, for it is a word, it is the word, for today. It is a word spoken to the powerful by those who have no voice but the voice of their suffering. And no one in this world has more right to be heard, more right to pass judgement, more right to call for a more humane future'– he was shouting now – 'no one has more right to be heard than those who suffer at the hands of those who idolize the ways of war. This' – he waved the letter above his head – 'this is the word which must be heard, above all others; for it is the word for today!'

He gazes round the hall. The silence is unmoved. But the word has been heard, and Jeremiah knows it. After all these years, he has not lost his touch.

Again the wife puts her hand on his arm. 'Jeremiah, the question is: Will the President listen?'

Her husband stands to let the prophet sit beside his wife. She repeats her question. 'Will he listen?'

Jeremiah puts his hand on hers. 'You have been hurt; and so you speak out. I was hurt. For more than twenty years I spoke out. I spoke words which burned my mouth as I uttered them. It was agony to me to criticise my own leaders in a time of crisis. Repeatedly, they said to me, "Watch what you say!" But God was forcing me to be subversive, whether I liked it or not. And the more I spoke out, the more I was hurt by rejection, by threats against my life, by imprisonment. In the end, when I was under house arrest, with the king poised to wage disastrous war, I put it all in writing.'

'Like our letter?'

'Like your letter.'

'And what happened?'

'They gave the text to the king – and the king burned it, page by page.'

'So what did you do?'

'I had it all written out again,' said Jeremiah, with a reminiscent smile.

'I think you are telling us that our words will fall on deaf ears,' says the husband.

'No!' says Jeremiah, waving his arm at the hidden audience. 'For these are not deaf; the world's suffering people are not deaf!'

'Nonetheless' says the husband, 'we must send this letter for the sake of our son, and,' – he bent towards the Afghan woman – 'for the sake of your little girl too.'

He is suddenly aware of someone standing at his shoulder – the old lady with the bright eyes, and royal blue headscarf.

'For the sake of my son also,' she says. 'He was murdered long ago; for the word which he had to speak.'

The king put more wood on the fire. It was dark outside now, the wind still heralding a storm. As he adjusted the logs he noticed a fragment of the document, still unburned on the hearth. Idly, he picked it up. He read: 'Do justice and righteousness. And do no wrong or violence to the foreigner, the fatherless and the widow, nor shed innocent blood in this place.'

The king sat staring for a long while, watching the flames consuming the new logs, as they might consume a tower in a besieged city. Then he crumpled the piece of paper and dropped it in the fire.

Wanted
dead or alive

Among many striking press pictures of September
11th was one of a young woman on a Manhattan
street, her body covered in dust from the crashing
tower. And, referring to Osama bin Laden, President
Bush said: 'There's an old poster out west...
"Wanted dead or alive."'

Anna – she'd chosen this new name for herself on the spur of the
moment – walked out of the store into a different world. She looked at
her reflection in the store window. She wouldn't have chosen those
clothes. But then she'd had no choice.

She'd staggered, choking and blinded, into the store, caked from
head to foot with a thick coarse gritty dust. The woman in the store,
with impulsive kindness and generosity, had given her water to wash,
had gently bathed her eyes; and then she had insisted that Anna
undress and change into new off-the-peg clothes.

And now new Anna in new clothes, with newly open eyes, walked
out into a new world. The great towers had collapsed. She had
imagined the initial impact, even the fireball, but somehow not the
sudden awesome concertina of the huge building, the dust cloud, the
running, the screams. At that moment she knew more than the police,
more than the firefighters, more than anyone else in the city, what had
happened. Perhaps she should have left the country before it
happened, but she didn't. She stayed, because that's what she'd been
instructed to do. And she had been wholly unprepared, for what had
happened – happened to her.

Far away, in another country, in a house in a village folded in barren
mountains, sat a group of men, their AK 47s beside them. They too

were impressed, as they watched the unfolding disaster on satellite TV. As replay of the crumbling towers followed replay, initial glee settled into steadily glowing satisfaction; the sort of satisfaction with which you might watch replays of your football team's spectacular winning goal.

Indeed, it was the work of their team, but it was not the winning goal. The deadly game was not over yet. It had hardly begun. The Great Satan would counter attack. They had planned for that. And a satanic attack upon their impoverished country would, they thought, give their next strike all the legitimacy they needed. And the girl, who had been indoctrinated with their hatred, their determination, their ideology, was their observer, hidden in the great city with the fallen towers. And so they waited.

In the city, an old woman waited also, in her apartment, for a knock on the door. It came. She opened the door cautiously.

'Abigail Judah?' asked Anna.

The old woman nodded kindly, and showed her in.

Anna began nervously. 'They told me you could help me,' she said.

Abigail smiled reassuringly. 'It's strange,' she said, 'you a Muslim girl coming to me, a Jewish woman for help. Come, sit down.'

'They told me you did it once… what I want to do.'

'Yes,' said Abigail. 'Something similar, long ago.' And in her memory she was young again, and beautiful, remonstrating submissively with an angry man, leader of a gang, on the hillside, a man planning a terrible revenge on her husband who had stupidly humiliated him. She recalled the thunder rumbling around the hill as she stood trembling in the face of the man's hostility. Why had she gone to see this David, whom till then she'd never even heard of? What had been her motive – to save her husband's estate from being torched; to save David, a would-be king, from an act of terror he would regret; or just to save her own skin? Even after all these years, she wasn't sure of her motives.

She turned to Anna. 'Times were simpler then.'

'Something inside me says I must… at least try,' said Anna, 'But I'm afraid.'

'I know.' The old woman took her hand. 'I read fear in your face – and courage too. I was afraid. Somehow I found the courage. And you'll need all your courage, my dear. You'll meet powerful men with made up minds. You'll be asking them to think again, in a crisis, when they most need to feel sure of themselves, least likely to listen to anyone – certainly not to a girl on her own – who asks them to think again. And you're going to try and show them a world beyond simple black and white, right and wrong, crime and punishment. They won't thank you. It's a terribly risky mission for you. You'll be on your own. They'll have all the arguments: and they have all the weapons.'

'Will you come with me?' asked Anna.

'Abigail smiled, hesitated, was about to shake her head. Then she said. 'Alright, I'll walk with you towards the palace.'

'They told me you were a queen, is that right?' asked Anna, as they walked.

'After my first husband died, I married a David. He became a king. So I suppose I was a queen – for a while, though I never thought of myself that way.'

They walked on in silence. Anna rehearsed to herself what she would say to the security guard at the big gates.

Abigail was back in her memory again. She could still feel the joy in her heart, and the relief, when David promised not to avenge her husband's brutish and unreasonable insult with a murderous raid on their estate. But that wasn't the end of the story. She hadn't reckoned on her husband's reaction. She thought she had saved him; as it was she destroyed him. She didn't know that she was going to bring her own world down around her. She thought of the TV pictures she'd watched, of that plane crashing into the city tower.

They turned the corner, and there was the palace.

'I'll leave you now,' said the old woman. She hugged Anna, and kissed her. Anna walked on alone, up the broad tree-lined avenue, towards the tall gates and the guards with their guns.

Meanwhile, in his great office, the President sat at his desk, preparing his battle plan. 'Dead or alive,' he said to himself. 'Dead or alive.' There was knock at the door, and the head of palace security entered.

'Mr President, sir, we're holding a young Muslim woman. She came to the gate. We've checked her out. We think she may have terrorist links.'

The President was angry. 'How the hell did she get through security?'

'She didn't, sir.' She came to the gate, alone. She's unarmed. We've had her searched.'

'Well, hold her,' said the president. 'You know what to do.'

'But Mr President, sir,' persisted the security chief, 'she wants to see you.'

'Me? A terrorist girl wants to see me?'

'Yes, sir. Says she has something very important to tell you; for your ears only, sir.'

'It's a plot.'

'No, sir. We have checked… '

'And she's alone? You're sure?'

'Yes, Mr President. Alone and unarmed.'

The president frowned, stood up, left his desk, walked to the window, and looked down at the great gates. The armed guards were there as always, and no one else, except a harmless old woman peering through the railings. 'Suppose,' he mused, 'just suppose… '

He turned to the security chief. 'Alright, bring her up here. I'll see her.'

The president watched the chief close the door behind him. Then he picked up the phone and called the head of his secret service. He paced up and down as he talked. His instructions were succinct and curt.

A few moments later Anna was brought in. She looked diminutive between two big armed guards. The President was sitting again. He stared at her. He thought her oddly dressed for a terrorist.

'What do you want?' he growled.

'To say I'm sorry, Mr President.'

'Sorry! Sorry!' the President roared at her. Thousands of innocents killed by your people, and you're sorry! Well it's too late for sorry.' He paused. 'Or too soon. When all your terrorists are dead and buried, then you can come and say you're sorry.' He spat the word back at her.

Anna, unnerved, repeated weakly 'Nonetheless, I am sorry.'

'And I'm busy' said the President. 'Take her away!'

The big guards escorted her to the door. In those few steps, Anna regained a little courage, and at the door she turned.

'Mr President, may I say just one more thing?'

'What?'

'Mr President, you are planning to attack my people. I can understand why. But if you do, more innocent people will die there.'

'And if I don't more innocent people will likely die here. Isn't that so? Your people are planning to strike again? Isn't that so?'

Anna lowered her eyes. She was silent; then 'I don't know. Maybe,' she said.

'Then maybe,' replied the President, 'maybe, I have the right, more than the right, the duty, to prevent them.'

'But,' replied Anna, looking up, gaining a little confidence, 'if you do strike at my people, Mr President, you give us an excuse to hit you again. And the violence goes on and on.' She could feel the passion in her voice. The president felt it too.

'So what are you saying?' he asked. 'That I don't punish the killers; that I let them get away with it? Where's the justice in that?'

Anna was silent. She remembered what Abigail had said about going beyond simple right and wrong, but she couldn't put what she wanted to say into words.

'Who sent you?' asked the President.

'No one sent me. I have come on my own, because I saw what happened to the towers and the people in them; and because now I believe with all my heart that terrorism, as you call it, is wrong; that it's wrong to kill innocent people. That is what the Koran teaches.'

'Huh,' said the President, looking hard at her, 'You've changed!'

'Yes, I've changed,' said Anna. 'But I'm only one person; a woman without power among my people. And you, Mr President, are a man, with great power among yours. And you could change too.'

'Go, just go!' shouted the President.

'Shall we hold her, sir?' asked one of the guards, as he steered Anna firmly towards the door.

'No,' said the President. 'Just get her out of my sight, out of the country. Send her back to her people. Let her preach peace to them.'

The guards led Anna out. The President sat back, satisfied with the intelligence opportunity she had given him. He had already given his instructions. Agents would follow her. Unwittingly she would lead them to the men who were pulling her strings.

Some days later, undetected by the President's agents, a burka-clad girl slipped into a house in the mountain village. The group of men sat inside, staring at her as she stood before them, staring in disbelief.

'You went to see the President, in his office? And you didn't kill him?

It was your duty, your holy mission! You were under orders!'

Anna could easily have said the obvious – that had she been armed she would never have got into the presidential palace. But that was not the point.

'I asked him not to retaliate.'

One of the men stood up quickly, AK 47 in hand, and made for Anna. Another restrained him. But all of them were speechless with fury. They glared at her with murder in their eyes. Anna felt their hatred, and her heart sank.

'This is treachery,' murmured their leader with menace in every syllable. 'You have abused our trust with treachery. And who has bought you? Who are you working for now? Tell us. Tell!'

'No one. I am working for no one!' cried Anna despairingly.

'We don't believe you!'

'I did it because I was there. I saw the suffering. And I knew it was wrong – wrong of us, wrong of the President. If you'd seen… '

'We see. We see very clearly. We see what you have done. You have betrayed your brothers and sisters, betrayed the world to which you belong. You do not talk to the infidel, you destroy him. And if you talk to the infidel you destroy us. Outcast!' they shouted. 'Outcast!'

In tears Anna rushed out of the house. Out of the village she ran, alone towards the bare mountain, weeping into a cold uncaring wind.

The men quickly persuaded a local mullah to issue a fatwah against Anna. Then they waited for the President to launch his attack.

Anna, hiding in the mountains, thought of Abigail. What happened to her? How was it that she married David, her second husband, and became a queen? Abgail had not really told her whether her peace mission had succeeded or failed.

Abigail, sitting in her apartment, thought of Anna. She thought of her first husband too. She could see him lying on the couch, drunk as usual, and, as it turned out, dying. She had told him what she'd done, how she had made peace with David. He, drunk too long on the spirit of vengeance, could not begin to understand. But he sensed she had left him – not left him for David – that came later, but left him in spirit. She had moved out of his world, and he could not follow her. She'd left him to die. She remembered walking out of the house, into no man's land, wholly alone between and old world and a new. And after all these years she was, she felt, still alone there – except perhaps for Anna.

Abigail wondered: would the men of vengeance, in the palace here, on the mountainside far away, ever be able to understand Anna? She feared not. Would Anna find peace for herself in offering it to others? Abigail hoped so. For she and Anna, separated by many miles and years, were kindred spirits.

Conversation
in the cockpit

US air attacks on the Taliban and al-Qaeda in
Afghanistan began in October 2001. US planes also
dropped food parcels. Several aid agencies criticised
the air drops of food parcels as an
ineffective gesture.

I was sitting in front of the TV. The last thing I recall watching was news pictures of poor and terrified people leaving Kabul to escape nightly pounding by US bombers. Where on earth are they going to go, I wondered, to be safe, and to be fed? Then I fell asleep. And I dreamt.

I was flying a plane – a big noisy transport plane. I was going to drop food parcels for those people. I flew straight and level, keeping my eye on the horizon ahead.

Suddenly I was conscious of someone sitting in the co-pilot's seat.

I froze. 'Hijacker!' I thought. 'Terrorist!' I sat rigid with fear. The man beside me said nothing. Slowly, I forced myself to glance at him. He was staring straight ahead. He was an old man, with white hair, and a white beard. A crazy thought went through my mind – Father Christmas!

'Aren't you going to ask me who I am?' asked the old man, still staring straight ahead.

'Well, who are you?'

'Moses.'

'Moses who?'

'Just Moses,' said the old man. He made it sound like a reprimand.

'You don't mean… the Moses?'

Then, in sheer relief, I said something really crass. 'I've read a lot about you.'

'So you should have done,' said Moses.

'What are you doing here?' I asked.

'I'm an adviser.'

'Advising whom?'

'Well just now I'm advising you. Look where you're going!'

I did. The sea was rushing up towards us. I corrected quickly. The plane settled down.

'That's better,' said Moses. 'Where are we going?'

'I'm delivering food parcels to Afghanistan. We're going to drop them from the plane.'

'Who told you to do that?'

'The President did.' I pointed to a notice on the cockpit window. 'The oppressed people of Afghanistan,' it said, 'will know the generosity of America and our allies. As we strike military targets we will also drop food to the starving and suffering men, women and children.' 'Those are my instructions,' I said.

'Food from the air,' said Moses. 'Do you know where that idea came from?'

'No,' I said. 'I suppose… '

'I thought you said you'd read a lot about me. Well, you should remember what you read. In the wilderness, hungry people? What did I do? I talked with God. He sent bread from heaven. No planes, no processed food, no preservatives. Fresh bread, delivered direct from heaven, six days a week for forty years.'

'So I'm really copying you. Isn't that good?' I felt pleased with myself.

'Steady!' shouted Moses. 'Watch your altimeter! No, you're not copying me,' he went on. 'Your motives are different. God said: "Set people free. Lead them to the promised land. Guide and feed them every step of the way." God's purpose was clear. Yours is confused. You drop bread out of one plane and bombs out of another.'

'That's right,' I said. 'Bombs for the terrorists, bread for the people. That's clear enough, isn't it?'

'It may be to you up here. It isn't to them down there. Do you know what they think? That at best you don't care about them, at worst you hate them. And every bomb you drop proves them right.'

'And every food packet we drop proves them wrong.'

'Not if you drop them from a safe height out of a warplane, in between bombs. The message of bombs contradicts the message of bread. You saw those people fleeing Kabul. They are afraid your bombs will kill them – with good reason. Do you think they see you as a friend? Your priority here isn't to feed the hungry, it's to destroy terrorists. You've told the world so.'

'But terrorists have declared war on America. Surely America has the right to try to destroy terrorism, to protect itself?'

'Of course,' said Moses. 'But who needs protection most? The country bombing or the country bombed? Which is worse, one day of war or twenty years of it? You are free; they are not. You're well fed; they are starving. To your way of thinking, you have reached your own promised land. Now help them find theirs.'

I said, 'We've promised to help the Afghan people rebuild their country after the war.'

'After the war's too late. Start now,' said Moses. 'Winter won't wait. Stop the bombing. Put troops in on the ground. Secure routes for food, medicine, blankets, aid workers, doctors. Make straight in the desert a highway for convoys. And look where you're going!' he screamed. 'Watch your altimeter!'

'Sorry,' I said as we climbed again. We were over Afghanistan now.

'Look down there,' said Moses. 'There's wilderness for you. I know about wilderness. I had to get them through it. With people wanting to go back, fighting, doubting, rebelling. But I knew I had to get them to where they belonged and feed them with hope along the way. It took forty years. But we did it. God made a free people of them. That's commitment for you. That's what those poor people down there are looking for – from you.

'And the terrorists?' I asked.

'Rich countries don't get rid of terrorists by bombing poor ones. You won't destroy them with bombs. Terrorism will die when people have respect, food, freedom, hope. It could take forty years. So start now. That's my advice,' he finished. 'And as I said, I'm an adviser.'

We were both silent. I looked down. I could see a large gathering of people on a mountainside ahead, and more joining them. Perhaps those people from Kabul were there, I thought.

'I'm going down to drop some food,' I said.

'Well go down carefully' said Moses. 'There's a big mountain just ahead. And remember what I said. Food dropped from a great height isn't as good as food brought, with care and commitment, along the ground. Your own aid workers are saying that, and they're right.'

We descended. We were low now. I could see faces looking up at us.

'Look at that!' said Moses. 'My successor's down there'

'Your successor?'

'Yes, you can see him in the crowd. He's down there, on the ground, feeding them already. All of them – five thousand I should say, at least. And I know him. That's just a start. He knows what long-term commitment means. And he knows what it costs.'

'Should I drop the food parcels, then?' I asked.

There was no answer. Moses was gone.

I woke up. The TV news had moved on too. Some economist was saying, 'UK consumer confidence appears not to have been damaged by the events of September 11th.'

Draining the swamp

On September 26th 2001, Donald Rumsfeld, US
Defense Secretary, said that the US objective after
September 11th was not just to get rid of bin Laden
and al-Qaeda but of all terrorists: 'The essence of the
strategy is to drain the swamp.'

It was a lovely autumn evening. The air was still; so was the water, as
far as could be seen across the great lake. The leaves of the trees edging
the lake, unmoving, hung fragile and golden brown in the low angled
sunlight. The wreck of an old boat lay by the lakeside, its timbers
casting an intriguing shadow on the surface of the water. A solitary
man stood beside it, looking out across the water towards the distant
mountains. Altogether, he thought, it looks like an evening I might
wish for as a calm ending to my life. And there was no obvious sign of
anything to disturb the sleep of the living.

But the man, as he walked home from the lakeside, knew he would
not sleep well. He had lived with that lake all his life. He'd noticed
changes. He saw what others would miss. He saw the transparent
husks of great larvae, remnants of a spring hatching, now clustered by
the water's edge under the trees. There had been none when he was
young; now they were beyond counting; a malign mutation, he
thought, the result of some corruption at work in the texture of
creation. And then there were the thin streaks of dirty yellow on the
water; like tiny trails of excrement, clearly visible in the setting sun. It
was perhaps a trick of the light, but on this evening the dirty yellow
streaks had seemed edged with many colours – like tiny parodies of a
rainbow.

The man shuddered at the thought. For he had lived his adult life by
faith in the rainbow. Old fashioned many might call him but Noah
believed that all creation hung on a single thread – a promise of 'never
again'. Never again, would God wash his hands of creation in an all-

destroying flood. He, Noah, had been chosen to ride that flood. He had stood again on good dry land. He had seen the rainbow sign.

What kept him awake that night was not doubt about God's commitment to the world, but about the world's to God. Men were again full of violence and violence had brought about the original flood.

Early next morning Noah walked down to the lake again. The air remained still, the water smooth. The rising sun had not yet climbed over the clouds on the mountains at the distant end of the lake. Noah knew what the clouds meant. They meant rain. He looked at the wreck of his ark at the waters' edge, and wondered how long the rain would last. He waited. A few leaves trembled and fell, early signs of a breeze. And Noah's mind was agitated, like a dove unable to settle on its branch but not knowing where else to go.

It lay dead in a sealed glass container. It looked like a giant dragonfly; but its wings were shiny black; and its body, not brilliant blue, but a dirty excremental yellow. On the front of its head was a long spike, like a sword. Death had not erased the evil look in its eye.

'So what do you want to do?' asked the senior biologist.

The defence chief continued to stare at the creature. 'No vaccine?'

'We're working on it; but nothing tested, nothing proven. That sword thing sure packs poison.'

'And it's suicidal – stings and then dies?'

'Sure; but that's not much comfort.'

'Risk?'

'Unpredictable,' said the biologist. 'Don't know where or when. But you've seen what a swarm can do. Can kill like hell. Thousands of people in a hour.'

'Why the hell do they do it?' mused the defence chief, half to himself.

'Programmed killers. Your only chance is to get 'em where they breed.'

'In the swamps?'

'In the swamps.'

'That's a helluva 'n undertaking,' said the defence chief.

'I know, but what else?'

The defence chief paced the room for a long time. Then, 'You know what?' he said.

'What?'

'We've gotta drain the swamp,' said the defence chief.

'Which swamp? They're all over.'

'Every goddamn swamp; the biggest first, where this bastard came from. We've gotta do it. To protect civilization.'

The mission was imperative. The death and destruction in the city had been bad enough. At first the authorities thought the damage was just physical – extensive and tragic, but containable. Then came the first signs of plague exuded by the unburned dragonfly corpses. People were scared, not knowing the extent of the danger. And the authorities did not know either, could not honestly reassure.

Operation 'Drain the Swamp' went confidently to begin with. The government of the Big Country was well equipped with sophisticated boats, pumps and hoses, and powerful disinfectants to neutralise the drained water. Other governments lent support. They and their people were genuinely sorry about the tragedy inflicted on people in the Big Country. Some also feared similar attacks.

The target swamp was in a country governed by rulers generally believed to be particularly wicked, and to be deliberately breeding the giant dragonflies in its swamp. The Big Country felt it had sufficient justification and support for an uninvited draining. And since this was not the breeding season, and neither dragonflies nor larvae were to be found in the swamp, a complete draining was the only solution. So a flotilla of boats, with pumps and hoses, moved in. The weather was dry and calm.

But the operation soon encountered problems. There were objections to the draining. For the swamp area, home to the terrorist dragonfly, was also habitat to many innocent, even benign, wild creatures, creatures that, because of their simple and austere lifestyles, were beloved by many humans, and considered by not a few to be positively inspirational.

Consequently, when increasing numbers of these treasured creatures were found dead above the waterline, people in countries whose governments were supportive of the draining, began to take to the streets in protests. Television companies made documentaries in which experts argued with each other about the efficacy – and the ethics – of the draining. Governments, initially supportive, became restive. And people were not convinced by the Big Country argument that the dragonflies were really the enemies of all creatures in the swamp country. Nor were they persuaded by Big Country promises to reconstruct the swamp when drained and disinfected; to turn it into an area for international tourism, with a great marina and much local employment. And there were conflicting reports about how far the water level in the lake swamp had fallen, and how long it would take to complete the draining.

Then the weather broke. It started to rain, hard and steadily, day after day. A blustering wind drove the rain into the faces of the drainers exposed in their boats on the swamp. And it was not long before the rain was filling the swamp faster than the pumps were draining it.

Clad in his oilskin, Noah came to the lakeside and waited. He would never have dismissed this expanse of water, in his corner of creation, as 'swamp'. After all, it was here that he had first seen the rainbow. But, as he stood in the driving rain, and saw the water now beginning to submerge the wreck beside him, awful memories flooded back. He looked at the remains of his ark. He looked up into the low opaque sky. He longed for a rainbow now.

And then far across the water he heard a mechanical sound. It was the engine of a powerful boat. Someone was coming. His waiting was over.

The boat emerged from the rain. Noah studied it. He reflected briefly on developments in marine architecture. He remembered the ark as it was, with its curved lines and then he looked at this angular machine in front of him, bristling with purposeful technology. The ark was for riding the waters, he thought, this vessel is for managing them. And as he climbed aboard, he noticed traces of yellow slime on its grey hull, just above the waterline.

'They said I'd find you here, sir,' said the commander, 'by that old wreck.'

'Find me?

The two men were sitting now in the commander's cabin. Noah had removed his oilskin. He felt ill at ease, his mental dove fluttering. But the coffee was welcome.

'Yeah. Our intelligence guys tell me you're the local weatherman.'

'Weatherman?'

'Well, maybe they were wrong. But you are some kind of guru? In touch with things here, for sure. And, sir, I need to know how long this rain's going on. I have to be open with you. It's preventing our operations. And it was not… not precisely anticipated.'

'I'm worried about the rain too,' said Noah.

The commander sounded relieved. 'Great! We're on the same side then.'

'I'm not so sure,' said Noah.

'But, sir, we have to destroy those monsters. They have killed my people. They are threatening… Surely you… ?'

'I know,' said Noah. 'Of course they are a threat. I have watched them multiply. I have lived with the danger. And I know about their attack on your people. And I am very sorry.'

'Then, sir, you must agree that we have to destroy this menace, to drain the swamp. Our mission is necessary. And the rain is preventing it. We cannot control the rain. And that is my problem. I have a duty to my government to solve it.'

'And are you asking me to tell you how to stop the rain? Is that it? I think you do not understand the rain. I have known rain worse than this, rain that has destroyed every human endeavour – seen it, and lived through it. And I think I understand now that man makes rain – this kind of rain – but man cannot control it.'

'So who is making this rain, sir? If I have that information, I can act. I can advise my government to open another front against the rainmakers. We can make a new game plan. We have satellites located way above the clouds… '

'Please,' said Noah, and there was a pause while he chose his next words carefully. 'I understand your passion, your determination to fulfil your mission, to destroy the cause of your people's suffering. But – and I hope you won't mind me saying this bluntly – I think that you and your operation are, in part, the cause of the rain.'

'Ah!' said the commander. 'You mean our draining operation has upset the local climatic conditions. I can call our meteorologists… '

'No, commander. That is not what I mean. Those dragonflies were bred in this lake, bred in resentment, bred to attack. Now you attack them in your resentment. And the rains come. The rains are waters of resentment. They refill the lake, and in the lake more resentment will breed next season. This has been going on a long time – attack and resentment, resentment and attack. The waters have been building up in the heavens for most of my life. And now I fear the skies can hold the water no longer, the windows of heaven open, and the rains come flooding down.' Noah hesitated. 'I have… I have lived through a global flood once before… and… '

'And?'

'And I am not sure that I – or you – will survive another. That is why I am worried, commander – deeply worried – about this rain.'

There was silence between them. Then the commander said: 'Sir my people have been attacked, have been wronged. My obligation is to destroy the attackers, to right the wrong. I believe in my mission, but,' and he pointed at the rain, 'I have a problem with it, as you see. Look at that rain.'

'Commander,' said Noah, 'I am trying to look through the rain, to see beyond it, beyond attack and resentment, beyond right and wrong. I know there is a better way. Once I saw a clear sign of it. I see no sign of it now. I must wait for it. When I see it again, through the rain, I will be able to show it to you. '

The Defence Chief sat at his desk. He put down the printout of the latest report from his commander of operations; he got up and walked to the window. He stared at the rain. He thought of the tornado now lashing at the south of his country. In the capital it had been raining heavily for days. He looked down at the ornamental lake outside the government building, swollen and distorted, overflowing the borders set for it by the architect, choosing its own level, finding its own shape. A lone bird, a dove, circled and circled over the water, unable, or perhaps unwilling, to land.

And Noah was standing by his lake, watching it steadily swelling under the pounding rain. The ark was nearly submerged now. And there was no sign of a rainbow. But Noah would wait.

Marjon's last journey

Marjon, the lion in Kabul zoo, survived over 20 years
of war. He was neglected, stoned, attacked with a
grenade. During the war in Afghanistan, the
International Society for the Protection of Wild
Animals tried to get help to Marjon, but the
lion died in January 2002.

Marjon padded up and down, trying to decide what to do.

The little bird, Ptica (Marjon pronounced her name 'Pteetsa')
perched on the torn wire mesh that served as a roof for Marjon's cage.
She stopped singing. 'Well, what are you going to do?' she asked.

'Dunno,' said Marjon.

Ptica was his only friend. Each day in the morning she came to sing
to him, and again in the evening. She was never far away. Most of the
other animals had died, or escaped from the zoo. None had had proper
food for weeks. There was no money to buy it. The keepers came when
they could, when they felt it safe, bringing scraps from the market.
Shells and bombs had blown cages open. Caged animals, deafened and
frightened, found momentary freedom. But it wasn't freedom really –
to leave a cage only to find yourself stoned by kids, shot at by soldiers,
terrified by bombing, and hungry to the end. The cages around Marjon
were all empty now.

Marjon looked up at the little bird, twisting his neck to see her
clearly, out of his one eye. He had lost the other when a man had
thrown a grenade at him. It was a revenge attack. Marjon, it is true, had
nearly bitten off the arm of the man's brother. But then Marjon was
very hungry; and the man was taunting him. War makes animals as
well as humans mad, thought Marjon.

Ptica was free. Unlike many songbirds, she had never been caged.
Marjon could not understand why she stayed around when she could
fly to the hills. Why did she keep circling and returning, every day? It

was as though she were attached to the great lion by some long invisible thread.

'It's safe to go,' said Ptica. 'I've been up to have a look. The city is quiet.'

Marjon looked at the door of his cage. It was secured only by a hook-shaped wire. Marjon could break open the door easily. But still he hesitated. He was afraid, as a prisoner at the end of a long jail sentence might be, afraid of freedom. He would not be safe outside. A half blind lion would look pathetic, vulnerable, even ridiculous. Yet to stay was dangerous too. The grenade man might return. And the gnawing hunger might never go away.

'I'll come with you,' said Ptica. 'I can see for you. From up here I can see everything.'

And she fluttered several metres into the air, singing her little song, to illustrate the point. Marjon followed her with his one eye as far as he could.

'I'll be your guide,' she said, as she settled again, this time at Marjon's feet, looking up at him from the dirt. She fluttered impatiently. 'Come on, it's getting late.'

And so, a few minutes later, the great wounded lion padded out of the zoo onto the street, slowly, carefully, afraid of what he could not see.

Children saw him. They screamed, and ran. Their parents ran too. A Toyota truck came careering fast along the road. The noise of it drowned Ptica's warning cry. The driver had seen the lion and was heading madly straight for Marjon. There was gunshot from the roadside. The bullet missed Marjon, hit the tyre of the Toyota. The vehicle careered off the road into a wall, and overturned.

Marjon ran. He ran down the long road. He did not stop running until he was out of the city. He sat by the roadside. He panted. He felt weak. And Ptica sat on the branch of a bush, at his side, where he could see her in the fading light. Marjon rested. Ptica waited.

'Are you ready to go on?' she asked after a while.

'Yes,' said Marjon gloomily.

'We must go up that mountain. Follow me.'

A young and healthy Marjon would have enjoyed bounding across the rough grass and sand, relished climbing a mountain, felt in command on its heights. But Marjon felt old, tired, hungry and lost.

'Come,' said Ptica gently. 'I'll be ahead of you, where you can see me.'

And so, slowly, in the dusk, the great lion and the little bird made their way up the mountainside together. The stars were coming out now. It hurt Marjon to twist his neck to look up at them. It was hard enough to see Ptica. But she stayed close. And even when he could not see her, Marjon knew she was there.

They reached the entrance of a cave in the mountainside. Marjon sat there to rest. The stars were easier to see from up here. But Marjon didn't look at them. He was studying the ground in front of him. There were human footmarks in the dust, fresh cigarette ends and a couple of Coca Cola cans. Marjon pawed the cans. Sugary liquid trickled out. Those cans had not been there long, Marjon could tell.

Ptica fluttered uneasily. Marjon sniffed the air. There was a scent of humans, faint, but, to a zoo animal, unmistakable. Men were coming, Marjon felt sure.

And Marjon was right. Two camouflaged men were making their way silently along the mountainside – now crouching, now crawling, intent upon the cave; drawn to it by their heat-sensing device, which had detected from afar the warmth of Marjon's great body against the night coldness of the rocks. Nearer and nearer, silently, stealthily they came, closing in on their prey.

The scent grew stronger. Marjon raised his head, and sniffed again. Ptica fluttered all round him.

The men were very close now, much closer than Marjon realised. One had night vision glasses. He crouched, focussing carefully on the cave entrance.

'Can you see him?' whispered his mate.

'It's not him,' said the man with the glasses, out loud. 'It's a bloody lion!'

Marjon turned and bolted into the cave. Ptica flew up the hillside. They were parted. Marjon ran alone into the dark, bumping blindly into the cave wall, first on this side then on that.

Then he stopped. There was no Ptica. And there was no sound but his panting. Marjon waited. Then slowly the tunnel ahead of him, not behind, took shape, in a dim, uncertain light. Marjon blinked. Moving fingers of light came stretching towards him along the uneven cave walls. Someone was carrying a lantern. Marjon heard men's voices.

And Marjon knew he was trapped – men behind at the cave entrance; men ahead in the tunnel. There was nowhere to go, nowhere to hide.

Terror seized him from head to tail. The men ahead were coming closer. In a moment they would see him. Marjon crouched. Two men rounded the corner. They carried guns, as well as lamps. Suddenly they saw Marjon.

Marjon leapt. With a mighty desperate, deafening roar, Marjon leapt and charged. He landed on one of the men, floored him, sunk his teeth into the man's neck. The other man stumbled, recovered – and shot blindly. Marjon felt the bullet rip into his thigh.

He let go of the man, roared and ran on, blundering down the tunnel. Then he stopped, as the pain in his thigh stabbed him. He turned, expecting the uninjured man to follow him, to shoot. But no one came. The light went. The men went.

And Marjon realised why. The tunnel led deep into the mountain. There was no way out but the way he had come. He would have to turn back, sooner or later. And all the men had to do was to wait for him, or barricade him in. He had entered his tomb.

He turned again, and limped on into the depths of the mountain. Broken thoughts came and went through his mind – of the scruffy zoo cage, of blue sky above its broken wire mesh, of little Ptica, singing and chattering – as he made his way into a captivity dark and final beyond his imagining. He limped on by instinct rather than intention, until he fell exhausted, and lay on his side.

Sometime later, he woke. It was still dark, still night. Marjon opened his one eye. He could see the canopy of stars spread above him. Slowly Marjon's mind cleared. Then 'Stars!' he said to himself. 'But… ' He sat up, wincing at the thigh pain. There was no doubt about it. He was sitting at a cave entrance, beneath the night sky.

His first explanation was that somehow the tunnel had led him round in a circle. He was back where he started. But then he looked for signs – the cigarette ends and Coke cans in the sand. There were none. There was no sand. Marjon limped forward a few steps. He was standing on thick fresh grass. A grassy slope, fell away before him. He thought he could see fields with low stone walls; and down in a valley a cluster of little lights burned, marking a village or small town.

Somehow, Marjon had made his way right through the mountain into a different world.

But he didn't feel safe. The terrors of this world were unknown. Marjon thought it best to stay where he was. He sat very still, under the stars. Then, suddenly, the night silence was broken by the bleating of first one sheep, then two or three more, from the hillside beyond the village. The sheep made Marjon feel hungry. He hadn't eaten anything at all since he left to zoo. But, 'Not yet,' thought Marjon. 'In a little while, safety first.' With that wound in his thigh he would not be able to walk far. Then he heard distant voices of men with the sheep. 'All men carry guns,' thought Marjon.

And now, in that great open space, he felt trapped by his hunger, pain and fear. 'Are lions always caged wherever they go?' he wondered, as he lay down hopelessly on the grass.

As he settled himself he noticed something. 'Just a few feathers,' he thought. But it was more than that. Marjon's heart thumped his chest hard. It was the body of a little bird. Gently he pawed it. The bird was dead. And the bird was Ptica. His little friend must have flown over the mountaintop, to meet and guide him again. She had exhausted herself beyond endurance in the cold, thin air. And now she lay at his feet. Marjon took the little body gently in his paws. His one eye watered, and a great big tear rolled down his furry cheek.

Then something very strange happened. Thinking about it afterwards, Marjon could not recall whether he was asleep or awake when it happened. But he was certain that it did happen. The little bird body lifted itself gently from his paws and hovered beside him; but it wasn't Ptica's real body. It was a transparent silvery shape of Ptica. But it was certainly Ptica. And then she flew up and up, singing her song. Then Marjon saw more little birds, all transparent, all silvery, rising from all around him; and yet more from over the hillside where he'd heard the sheep and the men. A great silver flock of birds was assembling between earth and the stars, circling and circling, growing as it circled, and singing.

One-eyed Marjon's vision was limited, but it seemed to him that the whole heaven was filled with a wonderful, slowly swirling translucent silver cloud.

Marjon felt the circling cloud of birds lifting his spirit, calling him to join them, calling him to follow, calling – so it seemed to him – the sheep, the men, calling everything to rise and follow. So painfully he stood up. He took a few stiff steps down the grassy hill. And the birdsong soothed his pain. His thigh hurt still, but not so much. Slowly and carefully at first, and then more easily, he descended. He found a rough track. He followed the track, followed the singing. And so he arrived at the edge of the little town.

It was still night. Candles and lamps shone through uncurtained windows. There were people on the move. And Marjon's fear returned. He was about to turn back, when a little girl crossed the road in front of him. She saw him. She did not scream or run. She stopped and smiled at him. Then he lost sight of her.

Two men stood at a street corner, talking. The men carried guns. Again Marjon hesitated. But the men did not move. They looked at Marjon with mild interest for a moment or two, then resumed their conversation.

People were certainly different here. And when, at the next corner, a man walked onto the road in front of him, shepherding two sheep and carrying a sickly lamb, the hungry lion felt no urge to stalk or pounce. Marjon knew that he was different too. And high above, the great tenuous silvery cloud of birds was still curling round itself, as though Ptica and her myriad friends were weaving a new mantle to cloak an old world. And their singing rained gently down upon the town, calling Marjon on.

He was aware now of being part of an informal untidy procession of animals. The sheep had been joined by cats and dogs, and two cows fixed him with a great bovine stare as he overtook them. There were geese, and deer with huge antlers, and a camel, then a donkey. The donkey was very thin, starving. Marjon noticed great weals on its back. And no one minded Marjon.

The little girl he'd seen ran past him now. In front of him she turned and, walking backwards, she smiled at him then, waving shyly, she turned again and ran ahead, looked back and waved again. Other children followed, and mothers and fathers trying to keep up with them.

A hope was taking shape in his mind now, a hope that there might, at the end of this procession, be something to eat and also somewhere to rest, for Marjon's thigh was hurting more now.

He reached the square at the centre of the town. It was crowded as for a fair. But there were no roundabouts, no big wheel, no music, just a great jostling crowd of animals and people. There was no sign of anything to eat. Marjon stood.

The square was brightening, as though someone were slowly turning up a great floodlight. Marjon twisted his neck to look up with his one eye. The bird cloud was condensing itself into a single revolving globe of transparent silver. And as it condensed the birdsong crystallised into a great harmony of many melodies, one for each animal and human in the square. Marjon clearly heard little Ptica singing high above, for him.

'Hello, Marjon,' said a voice beside him. He turned his head to look. It was the little girl again, smiling. 'Come with me. I've got something to show you.' Marjon thought the something might be food but he hesitated again.

'Come on!' said the girl, gently but impatiently, as though talking to a big family dog. 'Follow me.'

So Marjon limped after her. Fluttering with impatience and excitement, she made her way through the crowd as quickly as she could, turning frequently to make sure the lion was following, urging Marjon on. At last they were at the front of the crowd, in the corner of the square.

'Look, Marjon,' said the girl, pointing to a building.

Marjon looked. There was little to see. The building was much like the others, perhaps a little shabbier, with no windows but big double doors. The doors were wide open. There were more animals inside, and people – the shepherd with his lamb, and a young woman showing folk her new baby – and a great deal of hay and straw.

'Come on, Marjon! Inside.'

The lion followed. The straw looked comfortable, the hay smelled sweet. The starving donkey was eating it. An ox lay asleep, snoring.

'You can rest and eat now, said the girl.'

Marjon lay down by the ox. He smelled the hay. He nibbled a little. Then he took a mouthful, and another and another until he was full. Then he lay on his side. The little girl stroked his mane. She whispered something in his ear. But Marjon didn't hear. The great lion was asleep. The girl fetched some water, bathed his wound and bandaged it with a clean cloth. Then she kissed Marjon goodbye.

Marjon slept on and on. Dawn emerged from behind the dark

mountain. The silver globe dissolved slowly in light of the rising sun, and the birdsong faded. And Marjon slept on and on and on.

Down the years, in his new world, Marjon often told other animals the story of his last journey. He told it truthfully, so that, much as he would have liked to do so, he could not honestly say that he had really seen the baby. 'Not so as to remember it,' he would say 'But I'm not sure. As you see, I am half blind.'

My dream interview

On November 8th 2001, a Pakistani journalist interviewed Osama bin Laden at a secret location. Bin Laden said, among other things, that his mission was to 'spread the word of God, not to indulge in massacres'. At the same time the commander of US forces in Afghanistan said that the noose was tightening around bin Laden. Meanwhile, one option on the table for the political settlement of Afghanistan was to invite back the former king as a figurehead.

I am walking in the dusk along the road. Thick cloud hides the mountaintops, obscures the setting sun. Once the road was tarmac, but after years of war the surface is a patchwork of potholes. So, treading carefully in the fading light, I pass the rusting tanks and dusty refugee tents. It's a dangerous road. Fighting is supposed to have stopped here, on the road to the city. But gangs maraud still and there is always the risk of a bomb out of the blue, misguided by faulty intelligence.

I was told to come alone, and unarmed. And I am afraid, I admit it. But I'm a professional, a journalist. And I have the opportunity to meet the man at the centre of it all. He is a wanted man. The net is closing in on him, I'm told. I need my interview before it's too late.

My instructions are to be in the garden outside the city, at the foot of the mountain, at nightfall; to go there and wait. Well, now I'm waiting, in the dark, beneath the trees. I can't see or hear anyone. Very nervous, I lower myself against the trunk of an olive tree. It is chilly.

I sense that I am being watched. As my eyes become used to the dark, I'm sure I am. A small group of men, three I think, are sitting watching me – only a few metres away. Now I'm scared. I look back at them, our eyes mutually targeted. Slowly one gets up and walks towards me, almost gliding in the gloom, his long cloak brushing the dry grass.

'Come.' I join the three.

'Who are you?' I ask.

'We are members.'

'Where is he?'

'He has gone.'

'Gone? Where?'

'He will return.'

'When?'

'Soon. Please wait. Sit down – please.'

I sit with them. No one speaks, for a long time. I look at my watch. I have waited 20 minutes. I am increasingly tense. I'm beginning to think this is a trap.

'Where is he?' I ask again.

'He has gone to his prayers. You must wait.'

There is another long silence. Two of the men, I noticed, seemed to be asleep.

Now it dawns on me! He, the man I am risking my life to meet, has not gone to pray. He has just gone! He's no fool. He knows the danger he is in. He isn't going to risk seeing me. He's escaped, gone into hiding. I have lost my chance.

I turn to the third man again. 'He is not coming, is he?' There is no answer. The third man is asleep too. Their sleep confirms my suspicion. If they were expecting him they would be on guard, not sleeping cloak-wrapped on the grass. And I must stay with them. It's too dangerous for me to walk off alone in pitch darkness.

So I stretch out to try and sleep. And I am dreaming now.

I can feel the ground bumping beneath me. I'm in a jeep, wrapped in a blanket. I can see nothing out of the windows. They have been painted over. There's a screen between me and the driver. The journey goes on and on. By the movement of the vehicle and the sound of gear changes I sense we are climbing up and down twisting mountain roads.

At last the jeep stops. The door opens. It's dark outside. Two men grab and blindfold me. They guide me, firmly, silently, not violently, down what feels like a long slope. I sense we're in a narrow passageway.

'Steps,' said one, 'four steps, down.'

I feel my way carefully with my feet. A door closes behind me. One of the men removed my blindfold. I am in a small windowless room with plain rough plaster walls. A single lightbulb hangs from the ceiling. In the middle of the room are a cheap grubby round white plastic table and two chairs to match, and no other furniture.

On one of the chairs sits the man I have come to see. He is dressed, not as I had vaguely imagined, but in jeans and a leather jacket.

He and I are alone. The other two men have withdrawn, but I am sure they are just outside the door.

'Sit down, please,' he says.

I sit opposite him, and take out my notebook and pen. He looks at me steadily. His eyes are gentler than his reputation. I try to collect my thoughts, to feel professional.

'Well,' he says, 'I understand you have some questions. But let me ask you a question first. What are people saying about me?

I hesitate. 'Different people say different things'

'Go on.'

'Some say you are a threat to peace. As long as you're around, the focus of attention, stirring up the people, the infidel has every excuse he wants to destroy the nation. So, the authorities say, better they destroy you first.'

'And others?'

'Others think you stand for the true faith. They look to you to liberate the land from the infidel.'

'And,' I'm about to add, 'some say you are just plain mad.' But my words are lost in a heavy dull thud, which shakes the room from above us. Plaster and dust fall onto the table between us. A crack has opened in the ceiling. That bomb has surely buried itself into the mountain above us. The man looks up.

'Infidel at work,' he says, 'or liberator? What do you think?'

Uneasily, I take refuge in my role. 'I am a journalist. I am here to find out what you think.'

He smiles. 'Then you must ask your questions.'

I begin, referring to my notes. 'You are on record as forecasting that a tall building in the city would be reduced to rubble, and people heard you say openly that you would destroy it. Are they right to connect you with the attack on the twin towers?'

'I was misquoted – a little.' He smiles again. 'It does happen, with journalists, you know. But you must understand, I often speak in metaphor. I use words as windows onto truth. But I'll answer as plainly as I can now. I abhor violence.' Then after a pause, he adds reflectively, 'But when I see the powerful dominating the powerless from their towers and temples then, I admit it, I become angry.'

'But there are terrorists, or a least people with terrorist connections, among your close associates?'

'There are people from all walks of life among my associates. My mission is to spread the word of God. All who want to hear are welcome. I exclude no one who wants to learn the truth.'

'Do you plan to set the people free from the infidel?'

'The people are oppressed. There are warlords on all sides; like legions of demons, they have come from near and far. I would have them all driven into the sea like pigs. People need to be set free from the terror of war, and the hatred that causes war. Haven't you seen them in their thousands, by their tents, by the roadside, driven to the very margins of existence by war? But it is the truth, not the sword, that will set people free.'

'But surely you have a problem. You cannot convince people of the truth, as you see it, if you hide yourself away here. Yet as soon as you appear openly, you will be arrested, tried, probably executed – if they don't shoot you on sight, that is.'

'I know that.'

'But, forgive me,' I say, feeling a little frustrated, 'I'm not clear what you are trying to achieve. Stay here, and sooner or later they will probably get you. What can you achieve, hiding here?

'I am not hiding. I am biding my time'

'You may not have much time. They say the noose is tightening. What are you going to do?' I am raising my voice, my feelings getting the better of my professionalism. 'No one is sure what you stand for. Some say one thing, some another. They don't agree. You need to… to say something, do something, something clear, unmistakable. Otherwise you'll die a martyr or a criminal, and no one will be sure which.'

I think I may have gone too far. Now there is silence between us. The man looks down at the floor, then at me.

'You will know soon enough,' he says and then adds with his smile:

'You are not, I hope, going to suggest that I make a video for TV. That is the coward's way.'

'No.' And then I consult my notebook again.

'Abraham is the founding father of your faith; is that right?' I ask.

'Yes.'

'The other day,' I said, 'I spoke to someone who heard you say that you were greater than Abraham. Is that true?'

'I said it. But remember I speak in metaphor.'

'But then who are you? What do you plan to do? There's talk of bringing back the old king as a figurehead. Are you going to offer yourself as a new king of a new nation? You see yourself as a king?'

'If I said "yes" now, I think you would misunderstand and therefore misquote me.'

'But,' and my frustration surfaces now, and I am raising my voice, 'I can help you. People read my paper. It influences opinion. I can tilt things your way. I can do a little to set people free! Can you not tell me what you plan to do?'

'I must do the truth. Only the truth will set people free.'

'O for heaven's sake!' I shout. 'What is truth?'

There is another loud explosion, another bomb. This one wakes me. I sit up. One of the three men is standing over me.

'He's here – but hurry!'

I follow the man, stumbling between the olive trees, still half in the chimera of the dream interview.

And there, by the light of a swinging lamp I can see him. His prayers are over. He stands there tall in the lamplight. He looks shaken. Perhaps he has just seen someone killed by the bomb. The shadows thrown by the lamp make his face gaunt and inexpressibly pale.

Armed men come. He does not move. Two grab him by his arms, tie his hands behind his back. A third beats him on the neck with a rifle butt. They lead him away.

I turn my back. The clouds have parted now. By moonlight I can find my way onto the road. I walk back past the silent spectres of smashed tanks, the dismal low triangles of refugee tents.

'Why, O why,' I ask myself, 'did he not do something unmistakable, decisive, while he still had time?' Now he will die in ambiguity. His will be just one of many meaningless deaths in this playground of the violent.

The frustration of the interview returns. I would like to wash my hands of this man. But I can't, not now. I have to file my story.

In the cool
of the evening

On 26th October, Taliban prisoners attempted a mass breakout from a fort near Mazar e Sharif. An American military adviser called in the US bombers. It was reported that the bombers and Northern Alliance troops between them killed all the prisoners – several hundred. Journalists described the event as a 'bloodbath'. Mary Robinson, UN Commissioner on Human Rights, called for an enquiry.

I walked through the imposing but unmarked gateway, and up the long sweeping drive. I was carrying the day's newspaper. The mansion, I knew, was discretely hidden from the road. But as I reached the top of the rise in the land, there it was, on my right, an imposing russet brick building, old enough to be historic, new enough to be comfortable. And to the left, in front of the building, the long curving lawn descended to the orchard. This is the biggest orchard I know and late on this autumn afternoon every tree, as far as I could see, was laden with ripe red apples.

'Come and join us on the lawn,' said Eve, as she met me in front of the house. 'Adam's down there now. You haven't been to see us for such a long time! And what's the news?' she asked, taking the paper from my hand.

Adam was reclining on a sun lounger, facing the orchard and the late afternoon sun, contentedly munching an apple. Eve and I joined him. Eve had already started to absorb the news.

'This war in Afghanistan's terrible,' she said. 'Have you read about this bloodbath? Look, Adam, look at this picture.'

Adam ignored the proffered paper. He took a deep bite into his apple, and continued to gaze at the orchard.

'Got to be done,' he said. 'Terrorists would destroy civilization, like diseases would destroy those trees, if you gave them half a chance. Terrorists are a blight. It's them or us.'

'But all of them are our descendants. They're all our children and I'm… well I'm their mother. I hate to see my children killing each other.'

'They're my children too,' said Adam. 'But they're grown up. We can't be responsible for everything they do.'

'I'm not sure we've set them a very good example, brought them up as we should.'

'What d'you mean?' asked Adam, turning to her, raising his voice. 'We've set an excellent example! Look at all this.' He pointed to the orchard. 'When we started, this was wasteland – except for one single apple tree. Remember? And look at it now. We took one tree, one apple. We learned; we worked; we produced results. And now we enjoy the benefits. How to do that – that's what we passed on to our children. I'd say that's a very good example.'

'But look at this picture,' said Eve with some passion, holding the newspaper in front of him. 'Look! Where are the orchards in that picture? Where's the fruit of knowledge? Where did they learn to create a wilderness of war like that? Just look!'

Adam glanced at the paper, then brushed it aside and stood up. He turned to Eve. 'Woman, how long has it taken us to create this? Eh? How long? I'll tell you. A long time. One day those people will learn. And then we'll help them.' He took the paper from her, looked and pointed at the picture. 'See that? You see a wilderness there, don't you. Do you know what I see? I see an opportunity, an export opportunity! Imagine it, woman! Orchard upon orchard of Adam's Apples growing there, feeding the people, providing work! We'll make that wilderness blossom, woman. That's civilization. But first they've got to win the war, destroy the disease at the root. '

'So, the richest, most powerful nation in the world goes bombing one of the most destitute, weighing into a civil war that was brutal enough before. That doesn't seem very civilised to me.' Eve turned to me. 'What do you think?'

Adam contemplated the orchard again, but I knew he too was waiting for my answer.

'I'm no great moral authority,' I said.

'No,' said Eve, but you're one of our descendants. We need to know what you think.'

'You mean you want to know what he thinks,' said Adam.

'But I thought this was all about knowledge,' she answered tartly. 'You're always talking about everything being "knowledge based". Listen. You might learn.'

'Look,' I said, 'I don't want to start an argument between you two... '

'You've already started one,' said Adam. 'Now go on. Say what you have to say.' And he threw the core of his apple into a bush.

'I'm very grateful, we all are, for knowledge you've handed down, about how to create orchards and all sorts of other good things; though I must say that I think there may be more to civilization than orchards and export opportunities.'

'Like what?' asked Eve.

'Well,' I said, 'like having a sense of right and wrong.'

'We've got that,' said Adam. 'We got it through eating apples. And we handed it down to you.'

'Yes,' I said. 'But it's one thing to have a sense of right and wrong; it's another thing to know how to use it; to know what's right and what's wrong.'

'I should have thought it was obvious,' said Adam.

'Well, I don't think it is,' I said. 'You say the bombing is right. Eve thinks it wrong. And equally important, it's one thing to know what is right, it's another to do it. I sometimes feel you launched us into the world with a moral compass, but without a map and without much sense of direction.'

'Well, thank you for that,' said Adam. 'You seem to expect a lot of us. And you still haven't told us what you think about the war.'

'Right, I'll tell you. I think that you can't uphold civilization by uncivilised methods. And war is fundamentally uncivilised. Everyone who decides to fight, however just the cause may seem, takes a deliberate step back into barbarism.'

'I agree,' said Eve. 'And what you said about right and wrong makes sense too. We should have thought more carefully before we bit into that first apple.'

'You're a fine one to talk,' said Adam. 'You were the one who went scrumping in the first place! In any case, you're wrong. The problem isn't too much knowledge, it's too little – which is why I want expand this estate to include the tree of life.'

'But, Adam, you know the tree of life belongs to God,' said Eve.

'It may be negotiable,' said Adam.

I looked at my watch. 'I need to go,' I said.

Adam looked at his watch.

'Good heavens!' he said. 'Look at the time! God'll be doing his rounds in a minute. We'd better hide.'

I stared at them both in astonishment. 'You're not telling me God doesn't know… know about, about all this?'

'It's just a precaution', said Adam.

A week later I read about it in the paper – the great explosion. The bomb may have been dropped by a B52 or planted by al Qaeda terrorists. No one admitted responsibility. But the house was badly damaged, and most of the orchard destroyed. Amazingly there was no loss of life.

I phoned their mobile at once. Eve answered.

'God knows,' she said.

'You mean… ?'

'Yes, I mean he knows. We couldn't hide it from him any longer, could we? In any case, it was a pretence, a fig leaf. I think he's known for a long time. To be honest I'm glad it's out in the open.'

'So what will you do now?'

'Start again, I suppose. It's like being in that war photo I saw in the paper, you brought. Adam looked at it after you'd gone, you know. I caught him reading it. It will be hard work – like beginning all over again.'

After she'd hung up, I sat wondering. Would this be the beginning of a new story, or a repeat of the old one? With all my heart, I wanted us to go back to the beginning and start again, but how would we avoid repeating the same mistakes?

The moment
of truth

On the first weekend in December 2001, Hamas suicide
bombers killed 28 Israeli civilians in Jerusalem and Haifa.
Hamas claimed that these attacks were in response to the
Israeli assassination of a Hamas leader, and to the death
of Palestinian schoolchildren in a field booby-trapped by
Israeli soldiers. Israeli Prime Minister Sharon announced 'a
new war on terrorism...just as the US acts in its battle
against world terror with all its strength, so shall we do.'
US Secretary of State Powell said this was Palestinian
President Arafat's 'moment of truth'.

The two of them, old man and boy, sat on the hillside, on a low wall, outside the house. Evening was drawing in. The old man was pointing to the rocky and still sunlit hilltop beyond the shadowed valley.

'The Great Battle was fought down there in the valley,' he said, 'where the city stands now, but it was on that hill over there that, the night before, the king prayed for victory.'

'Our king?'

'Yes. The story's in The Book. The king prayed, "God save your people, and grant us victory." But a messenger from God visited the king and said: "O king, ask not for that which cannot be given. Your reign is at an end. For though you are powerful and rich, your people are hungry and poor. You have been blind to their need, deaf to their cry. Therefore is God angry with you. He will take away your kingdom and give it to another."'

The text was engraved on the old man's memory. He went on.

'The king pleaded with the messenger. He promised to share his wealth. But the messenger was stern. "God in his time will send the people a great and just leader. But your time is past; tomorrow is your defeat. Henceforth for many years shall foreigners rule this land."'

'And what happened, grandad?'

'There was a terrible battle. Many were killed. The story says the river down there ran red with blood. And our king was defeated and this land was occupied by foreigners, as the messenger said.'

'And did the great just leader come?'

The old man stared absently at the horizon. He shook his head.

'Not yet,' he said quietly.

The two were silent. The old man looked down on the city. There was enough light for him to see the straggling shanty town, the city's open wound, at one end, and at the other, the great tower block, symbol of new foreign investment, adorned with an illuminated multinational logo. Then he turned to the boy.

'Do you ever long for something you can't put into words?'

'I don't know. I don't think so.'

'Our land is not just the place where we live. It's a dream; the dream is as old as the land itself. It's a dream of things as they should be, of a people at peace with itself, with the world, with its God. It's our dream, yours and mine.'

The boy, puzzled, did not know how to reply. So he said: 'I'm getting cold, grandad.'

The old man removed his cloak and wrapped it round the boy's shoulders, hugging him as he did so.

'Here, take this. And the dream with it.'

'Thanks, grandad.' The boy smiled up at him.

And they talked of football, school and other things, until it was time to go indoors.

The new prison was built into the side of the hill on which, long ago, the king had prayed for victory. Its barred windows looked down on the city below. Standing by the window, the prisoner heard the city sounds but he, the most famous, or most notorious, prisoner in the country, saw nothing.

For Samson was blind. Or at least he said he was. He wore a bandage over his eyes. He claimed that his captors had blinded him in torture. They, on the other hand, claimed that he was not blinded, but simply blindfolded.

It would of course have cleared the matter up if either Samson or his guards had removed his blindfold. But Samson would not remove it. His guards, under instruction from the chief of police, would not remove it either. It suited Samson and his followers to maintain that his captors had gouged his eyes out. It suited his captors to maintain that his blindness was self-imposed. Confusion about Samson's sight served to sustain hostilities. And hostilities were not over. The president in his palace knew it. Samson in prison knew it. And Samson confined had plenty of time to think about his incomplete mission, about his trial, about what he saw as his destiny.

His grandfather had never asked for his cloak back. Samson the teenage student had little use for it. But Samson the ambitious militant dissident in his twenties found it in a cupboard one day. And the next day he discovered its power.

It was the day of the great demonstration against the foreign airbase. A big crowd had gathered in the city square, outside the palace, in front of the nation's Monument to Justice. This was a classic figure, with sword in one hand and olive branch in the other, and an imperial cloak draped over its shoulders. Samson had brought his grandfather's cloak. He stood in the crowd with Saul, his political confidante since university days, listening impatiently to the speeches. Then with a sense of symbolic timing and gesture, which soon became his hallmark, he chose his moment.

'Now' he said to Saul.

Saul nodded, patting Samson on the back, pushing him forward.

Samson broke through the crowd. He mounted the steps of the monument, trailing the cloak behind him. He positioned himself carefully, immediately below the statue, and faced the crowd. He raised the cloak high for all to see, then lowered it onto his shoulders.

No words were needed. The young man, hitherto an eccentric extremist with a small following, became overnight the acknowledged leader of the zealot network, and the man most wanted by the secret service.

The demonstration against the foreign airbase was not an isolated protest. Samson, Saul and many others saw it as the latest and most offensive manifestation of the occupation of their country. The governing elite, corrupted by the prospects of wealth and privilege set in concrete, had invited tower blocks of foreign investment. With the tower blocks came foreign technocrats living tax-exempt lives in luxurious compounds. And the technocrats brought their alien culture – music, videos, magazines and fast food, all available in city shops. And then, beyond the sprawling, growing, neglected shantytown, came the airbase, the result of what the government called a mutual security pact.

Samson was leader. But Saul, the lawyer, formulated zealot ideology. The historic defeat of the nation, he argued, was being repeated, not by conquest, but by invitation. The government was not only unfit to govern, it had no right to govern. It had betrayed the nation's destiny. It must be removed, by revolution if need be. The day of the just leader had dawned. Land and people must be purified, said Saul, and his own austere religious lifestyle showed what he meant. The time had come to level mountains and valleys and straighten crooked things. Influenced by Saul, Samson thought he understood his grandfather now. The age-old dream was in his head, the cloak upon his shoulders. He would recall the nation to its destiny, redeem the present for the sake of the future.

Samson and his zealots had much public support, especially in the shantytown, for their declared ends; enough support to provide cover for their means of achieving them. Their first assassinations were quickly followed by arrests, arrests by shoot-outs on the streets. Police in turn shot, slashed and burned their way around the shantytown, destroying indiscriminately, trying to smoke out the zealots. Anxious about its airbase and its investments, the foreign power provided military advisers and weapons. The government accepted both. The zealots in turn acquired more popular support – and more explosives.

Men of violence battled to control the city. On the one side they inhabited the back streets, hid behind false identities, kept their plans secret. On the other, they wore uniforms, drove armoured vehicles, gave press conferences – and hunted Samson. They wanted him dead or alive.

And in the end they caught him – in a honey trap. Zealots had just blown up a car killing five foreign diplomats on their way from the airbase to the palace. Saul at once went into hiding, to pray and fast, as was his habit. But Samson, flushed with success, incautiously decided to celebrate in a small restaurant in a zealot-friendly neighbourhood. There he wore his cloak. And there he met Delilah. Samson had a weakness for beautiful women, like his weakness for gestures. He took

Delilah to bed. She was a secret agent. By morning the restaurant was surrounded by police. They bundled a blindfolded Samson into the back of a jeep. His cloak disappeared.

Later that day TV cameras followed his progress up the hill to the prison, in a sealed van. By evening the world knew that a sightless, cloakless Samson was behind bars. The mystery of Samson's eyes began. And the world waited for his trial.

The day before the trial, there was a funeral in Samson's home village on the hillside. Many came, for the old man had been much loved in the hill country.

Country folk had watched the city in the valley becoming more brash, more greedy and now more violent. They were afraid of the new world coming to birth below. The old man, with his love for The Book and its stories from the past, had seemed to them to be the last custodian of a vision of a better life, liveable now, if at all, only on the sunlit hills.

It was evening. All but one of the funeral guests had left the house now, a young man wearing dark glasses. The old man's daughter, sitting by the window, looked up at him, trying to read his expression.

'Does he ever talk about his grandfather?' she asked.

'Sometimes,' said the young man; though 'never' would have been nearer the truth.

'They used to spend hours together sitting on the wall out there. He'd tell the boy stories. And they'd talk about football.'

The woman started to cry.

'It broke his heart when Samson… ' Her tears overwhelmed her. '... and now I have lost my father as well as my son.'

The young man removed his glasses and drew up a chair beside her. He was a little embarrassed, for he hardly knew the woman. He hesitated, tentatively took her hand, just for a moment, and then let it go.

Nothing was said for a few moments. The woman wept silently now, face down. The young man looked out of the window, waiting for her tears to subside. Then, with her head still bowed, the woman said:

'Do you think you could do something for me, for father?

'I'll try, of course.'

'Could you give this to Samson? I know his grandfather would like him to have it.'

From the window ledge she took, and gave to the young man, a well-thumbed copy of The Book.

'It would mean so much to me to be able to think of Samson reading it as his grandfather used to read it to him.'

The young man turned the pages at random. He noticed many passages carefully underlined in red ink, with notes in the margin.

'I'll try,' he said. 'But it won't be easy. I can't go to the prison, not now.' And to himself the young man thought that Samson probably wouldn't want to read The Book anyway, at any rate not now, the day before the trial.

'Of course. I understand. But do please try.'

'I will.'

'And has he still got the cloak?'

'I don't know.' This was scarcely true, for he was pretty sure that it was in the hands of the chief prosecutor, who would no doubt make full use of it.

It was dusk as Saul left the house, putting his dark glasses on again. He felt troubled by the book he carried and by Samson's mother's request. He wished she had not made it. He stopped and looked down into the valley but it was too dark to see the presidential palace where the trial would begin the next morning.

He walked down into the city, through dark and narrow back streets, and up the hill on the other side. He stood among the rocks above the prison. And then Saul, The Book in his hands, knelt on the rocky ground, under the stars, and prayed for victory. As usual, he was clear about what to pray for, and against. But that night, as soon as he started praying, familiar moral landmarks began to move around inside his head, like stars above drifting from their known positions. He was losing his bearings, losing control of his prayer. The prayer was taking control of him. He was battling with someone else inside his head, battling and losing. His wounded spirit cried out among the rocks. And above him the stars were forming a new map of the universe.

The next day, the trial was spectacular. Almost certainly, the investigators concluded afterwards, security staff at a very high level must have been covert zealots. Otherwise it could never have happened.

Four huge explosions in quick succession blew the courtroom apart. Sixty-five people were killed, including the trial judge, the chief prosecutor, three government ministers among the spectators, and several security guards. Samson's body was crushed and charred almost beyond recognition. The truth about his eyes died with him.

The explosions also blew a great hole in the frontage of the palace, and hurled the cloaked figure of justice down the steps. Sword and olive branch became one with the rest of the rubble.

Weeks later, Samson's mother received a letter. The stamp was foreign, the handwriting unfamiliar.

> 'I knew what was going to happen at the trial. And as I prayed on the hill the night before I suddenly knew it was wrong. But by then I could do nothing to prevent it.
>
> Our government was unjust, in all sorts of ways. It still is. But I was blind. I could not see my sense of justice was really a cloak for my intolerant self-righteousness. And with that, I encouraged Samson to destroy others and to destroy himself.
>
> Am I asking too much, to ask you to forgive me, who has been so unforgiving of others, who has destroyed your son?
>
> I still have your father's copy of The Book. Do you want it back? I read it a lot. You know the story of the Great Battle, and the messenger who promises that God in his time will send the people a great and just leader? Well in the margin your father wrote in red ink "We need more than justice."
>
> I wish I could ask him what he meant. You see, I think if we are ever to redeem the dream we need a leader with the imagination to transcend our ideas of right and wrong. Otherwise we will keep building things up, only to pull them down on top of us.
>
> There are people from many countries in this city. I talk to them about these things.'

Samson's mother put down the letter and looked out of the window. For a moment she could see again the old man and his grandson sitting together on the wall overlooking the valley, talking, imagining. Then she could see no more, for her eyes were blind with tears.

The four wise men

Just before Christmas 2001, Israeli Prime Minister
Sharon banned the Palestinian President Arafat from
attending the Christmas night mass in Bethlehem,
which he had attended in previous years. President
Arafat declared this 'a crime depriving me of my right
to participate in the commemoration of the
messenger of peace.'

It was midnight when they came to the crossroads. They had come a long way, these rulers. Word had reached them of a new peace initiative, right at the heart of the land of intractable troubles. They hoped this initiative, whatever it was, might be something they could copy, to conquer the destabilising forces which so troubled their own lands – ethnic violence, tearing the heart out of already impoverished communities. The three kings had come along way; and now they were at the border of their destination. Clouds hid their guiding star so, unsure which way to go, they decided to camp by the crossroads for the night.

When they woke at dawn there were four of them. The three were not unduly surprised. After all the original story did not specify a party of three, or any other number for that matter. Nonetheless, they thought it sensible to establish the credentials of their new companion. This was after all, as they saw it, a high-level peace mission. Its integrity must be safeguarded.

'Are you a wise man?'

'Years of struggle have made me wise.'

'Are you a king?'

'I am the chosen leader of my people.'

'Are you armed?'

'No.'

'Why do you wish to join us?'

'I want peace for my people in a state of their own.'

'Do you know the way to Jerusalem?'

'Yes. I will show you.'

'Then you are most welcome to join us,' they said.

Their new companion was rather pleased to be accepted by these figures from the wider world; pleased for himself, for his status needed a boost just now, and pleased for his people.

They rode on together. Outside the city they stopped. It was time to put on ceremonial dress for their audience with King Herod. The fourth, not having suitable clothing, asked if he might borrow spare garments from the others. They agreed, thinking that the dignity of the mission as a whole justified a minor deception over the appearance of one of its members. It would do no harm.

So, resplendent they all looked, mounted on fine camels, as they road up the main thoroughfare towards the palace. They were crowned with ornate turbans, enveloped in long robes – maroon, royal blue, green and orange – all magnificently embroidered with gold. In front walked the commander in chief of Herod's army who had greeted them at the city gate. On either side people pressed themselves against walls and traders' stalls, to allow the great ones to pass.

The procession halted at the palace gate. Herod's chief minister was waiting. The commander saluted him.

'Commander!' whispered the minister.

'Yes, sir.'

'I thought there were only three of them.'

'There are four, sir.'

'I can see that, commander,' said the minister testily. 'Where is the fourth one from?'

'I don't know, sir.'

The gates were open now and the four dignitaries passed through. The first minister eyed them very carefully. He was especially interested in the fourth one, clad in orange. The minister continued to scrutinize him as the audience with the king got under way.

Protocol, and security, required that the visitors sit at some distance from Herod on his throne. This made conversation difficult. The orange guest remained silent, his head down, the brim of his turban hiding much of his face, as the other three explained to the king the reason for their journey.

'I am king,' said Herod loudly, to hide his consternation. 'There is no newborn king of the Jews. You have been misinformed.'

But as he spoke, very disturbing thoughts were already chasing each other inside his ever-suspicious mind. 'New king born' probably signified the start of another revolt; possibly an attempt on his life. He was used to missions of misguided woolly liberals from the West trying to get him to make peace with terrorists. But these were from the East, probably fundamentalists in disguise, with 'star' a code name for some international terrorist network. It was all horribly clear. Why had his intelligence service not picked them up at the border? How had they been allowed to penetrate the palace? Had they been searched? If not, why not?

Herod hid his mounting alarm. He played for time.

'Minister!'

'Your majesty?'

'Come here!'

'Your majesty.'

The chief minister approached the throne, and bowed.

'Go and find out,' said Herod in a loud voice, 'if we have any reports concerning a birth in our extended family.'

And then he added in a whisper, 'By which I mean, minister, any new terrorist intelligence. And tell the head of security to search their baggage – at once, and be prepared to detain them!'

'Your majesty,' said the chief minister, as he bowed and backed away.

Herod, apparently amiable, turned to his visitors as the minister left the room. 'Tell me about the political situation in your kingdoms. I like to learn. Tell me.'

Each in turn, the first three spoke. Then Herod turned to the fourth.

'And you, sir? What of your land?'

The orange-clad visitor raised his turbaned head. The king stared hard at his face. Then the chief minister re-entered.

'Ah!' said Herod, diverted. 'What news?'

The minister approached the throne briskly.

'Bethlehem, your majesty. There is information about a royal birth in

Bethlehem.' And the minister nodded as he spoke.

Herod read the nod. A revolt, a terrorist attack planned for Bethlehem, he thought. Bethlehem, a royal birth in the royal city and now 'royal' foreigners in his palace! The connection was unmistakable. It was an international conspiracy. His throne was in imminent danger.

But Herod was no stranger to bluff, subterfuge and conspiracy. He was foxy. He would outmanoeuvre his visitors.

'Ah! Bethlehem, of course!' he said, expansively. 'That is good news. Forgive my absence of mind. Please, go to Bethlehem by all means. Be my guests. My staff will accompany you. Visit the child. It is my privilege that foreign heads of state be the first to pay respects to a… a, let us say, possible future king. And when you return here inform me, no advise me, then I will go to city and pledge myself to serve my peoples' future.'

And to the minister he whispered, 'And tell the commander, make sure they are watched every step of the way.'

'And now you must go,' he continued loudly to the visitors. 'I bid you farewell.' Herod stood and stepped down from the throne.

Each visitor in turn walked forward to shake hands with the king. With the first three Herod's handshake was perfunctory. He was anxious to be rid of them. But to the fourth he said, 'Please wait one moment. I would like a further word with you.'

The other three overheard the menace in his voice as they left the room. The minister closed the door behind them. Herod and the fourth visitor were alone now.

'Take off your turban,' commanded Herod. The man hesitated. Herod ripped the orange turban from his head.

'I knew it!' shouted Herod, triumphantly, hurling the turban across the room. In his own mind his suspicions were fully confirmed. 'I knew it! How dare you enter my palace like this!'

And then, through the closed door, he yelled: 'Chief minister! Come at once!'

Immediately the minister entered.

'Fetch the commanding officer.'

'Yes, your majesty.'

And the minister went again, closing the door after him.

Confronted by a fiercely angry Herod, the man was not unnerved.

'You and your soldiers have denied me any normal means of

communication with you,' he said. 'This was the only way I could get to you.'

'You communicate with me?' roared Herod. 'I will not communicate with you. You are a terrorist. You condone terrorism. I will not speak with a leader of terrorists.'

'I am the leader of a people whose rights you deny, who seek a peace which you will not give. Is it surprising that the desperate among them turn to terror? I do not condone terror. But I alone cannot prevent it.'

The minister re-entered, with the commanding officer.

'Commander!' shouted the king. 'Have this man escorted to his hometown; place him under house arrest. I want a 24-hour guard on him.'

'Yes, your majesty.'

Then the minister said: 'Your majesty, what shall we do with the foreign visitors? They are waiting outside.'

'They will go to Bethlehem. I am grateful to them for the information they have brought,' he said pompously, as though addressing a full council of ministers. 'It enables me, enables me to announce a new peace initiative in Bethlehem. It will be called,' (Herod chuckled), '"Operation Royal Birth". I want Bethlehem surrounded, all terrorists suspects arrested, and all movement in and out of the city stopped.' (He chuckled again.) 'I will give my foreign friends a lesson in peacemaking. Let them go to Bethlehem and see how we keep peace in our kingdom.' And turning to the fourth visitor, he added: 'And take that ridiculous robe off.'

The man ignored the remark. 'My people are in Bethlehem. In a crisis I have a right to be there with them.'

'Right!' roared Herod. 'You have no right to be anywhere but in your own house until I am satisfied that you have eradicated terrorism from the land. And if you don't do it, my soldiers will do it for you. Take him away.'

The commanding officer escorted the man from the room.

'Your majesty,' ventured the chief minister again, 'Why does your majesty not arrest and imprison him now?'

'What?' said Herod, 'and hand his people an excuse for an immediate terrorist attack in Bethlehem before I have the city under total control? I know what I am going to do.' And that was true. He had already made up his mind.

The three kings rode on to Bethlehem, saying little, but doubting their wisdom. They realised now that their fourth companion had been less than open with them. He had used the borrowed orange robe to cloak more than his shabby clothes. Herod, it was obvious, was even less to be trusted, and more powerful. His menace accompanied them to Bethlehem, as an excessive number of his armed guards rode close and silent beside them. Their peace mission, they felt, was compromised now. They had hoped to find a solution. Now, it seemed, they had allowed themselves to be dragged into the problem. And they wondered whether the bright cold star, which had reappeared low in the sky ahead, was not perhaps silently mocking them.

They entered the city. It seemed to them, a sullen, tense militarised place. They came to a square. It was empty, presumably under curfew.

The officer of the escort stopped. He seemed as uncertain as the three kings as to what would happen next.

'We wait,' he said, curtly, and made it clear that he would say no more.

And they waited. After a few minutes the kings dismounted their camels. They strolled a little, to stretch their legs. They whispered to each other their annoyance with the guard, their frustration over their mission. There was no royal birth in this place. The officer, unable to overhear, watched them carefully.

The door of a tiny dwelling in the corner of the square opened. A young woman came out. She was poorly dressed. She approached the party. At once soldiers moved and made to bar her way. The kings watched the woman, and the soldiers. Then, 'Let her come,' they said, firmly.

The officer sensed the authoritative tone and, conditioned to obey commands, he motioned his men aside.

'Please come to the house,' said the woman. She was overawed neither by the regal bearing of the visitors, nor by the soldiers. She spoke with both gentleness and confidence in her voice. 'Come, please.'

It took the kings a moment to realize that she was inviting them, not the soldiers. They followed her to her door, surrounded by their guard.

'Please come in,' said the young woman smiling.

The kings firmly indicated to the officer that he and his men should wait outside. Then they entered the low door, bowing their heads.

The room had little furniture, few personal belongings. It was more like a place for waiting in than living in. But in one corner was a cradle. From the cradle the woman gently lifted her baby. She held it in front of the three and, as she did so, she parted the folds in its shawl, to reveal its face. Its tiny eyes were open.

'Look!' she said, though she did not need to, as the three men were already staring intently at the child's face. 'My son.' The kings looked on at the child, in silence, for what seemed to the mother a long time. Then, kindly, they looked at her.

'You must go, you and the child, you are not safe here.'

'I know; but we have no money. My husband and I are poor.'

The kings looked at each other. The same thought came to all three at once.

'Here, please take this,' said one, as he placed the gold coins on a little table. The others placed their gifts. 'You will find uses for these, too,' they said.

The woman said nothing. But she smiled her gratitude, and then bent her head towards the child in her arms. The kings were slightly embarrassed. This was not what they had imagined or planned. Their gifts, intended for royalty, seemed not quite appropriate.

'We must go,' they said. And they left.

Outside the door, the officer was menacingly interrogating a young man, obviously the woman's husband returned.

'Let him in,' said the kings.

The officer did so but he was very uneasy now. He could not get it out of his head that, unlikely as it seemed, somehow this whole encounter had been prearranged.

The kings stood in the square. They looked at the sky. The star was no longer visible. Then they issued their final command.

'We wish to leave your country, at once, by the shortest route. Please show us the way.'

At the border they dismissed the guard. The officer rode off, wondering how he should explain things to his commander.

The kings rested a while and reflected. They had seen in the face of that baby boy something that they, preoccupied with power in their unstable world, needed to see. And they were not the only ones in need of this vision.

Their fourth companion was now presumably under Herod's guard somewhere. But he should have come with them. They should have insisted on that. He should have set aside his preoccupation with his rights, stopped cloaking his intentions. He should have come to Bethlehem, not because he was entitled to be there, but because he needed to be there.

And Herod too, he certainly needed to step outside his panoply of power, to suspend the ranting which cloaked his chronic insecurity and fear. He should have come with them. He needed to see what they had seen. For what they had seen had moved them deeply. They did not know whether to fear or hope for that child's future. They only knew his future mattered to them.

Soon after they returned home, travellers brought them word of 'Operation Royal Birth'. From his palace, Herod had ordered the systematic slaughter of all the baby boys in and around Bethlehem. In their respective palaces, each of the kings remembered sadly and wondered whether the child, their child, had escaped. They very much hoped so. And they hoped their gifts might have helped in some way.

Execution on video

The Wall Street journalist, Daniel Pearl, was abducted in Pakistan on January 23rd 2002. A month later a Pakistani journalist received a video of Pearl's execution, apparently by terrorists. Pakistani authorities charged a British terrorist suspect in connection with Pearl's murder. Daniel Pearl's wife, Mariane, said, 'The terrorists 'may have taken his life, but they did not take his spirit. Danny is my life... they did not take my spirit.'

John said, 'Come round for supper,' and I said I'd be glad to. I know John and Sue well, and anyway I wanted their advice. We ate, then I helped clear the table, though with one hand still fully bandaged I avoided carrying anything heavy or fragile.

'Refill your glass,' said John. 'Bring it into the lounge.'

I settled in the armchair, and sipped.

'This is an excellent red,' I said.

'Now,' said Sue, 'tell us about the programme and the man you interviewed and what happened after. Did you see the whole of that awful video?

'Of course. And it was nasty.'

'The bits you showed were revolting enough. It was sick... '

She was of course talking about that TV documentary I'd made, which had made news, and become controversial, partly because of the clips from that execution video. Predictably, we were bombarded with critical viewers' letters about that: 'degrading'; 'disgusting'; 'a gratuitous and unforgivable offence against public decency.' A few called us 'courageous' and some wanted to know more about the victim – who he was, why he'd been killed.

We didn't show the worst bits in the programme, naturally, just long shots of the dying man's face, and only a hint of the blood. It was a pretty amateurish video anyway, with the camera waving about all over the place, obviously being jostled in a crowd. You could see one or two of them baying for blood, but most just watching, still and silent. There was a close-up of one woman weeping. I found out who she was later.

I didn't really want to see even the edited footage again, at least not this evening, not with a glass of red wine in my hand.

'I'll just play you the interview,' I said, 'as much as we saved, anyway.'

'What was he like,' asked John, 'the man you interviewed?'

'Enthusiastic, eloquent, hard to pin down, hard to make out.'

'Where exactly did you interview him?'

'In the suburbs,' I said evasively. And I thought of the dull shabby house. It could have been anywhere. The gunmen knew where it was, though. I felt my bandaged hand.

I slotted the tape into the player beneath the TV and pressed the start button. The picture flickered and then settled. There he was: small, intense, sitting opposite me, oblivious to camera, light and mike, just determined to talk and talk.

'What's different since September 11th? I'll tell you. We've been pitched into a new 'them and us' world. Just listen to the rhetoric! One side defines Western values in terms of the global defeat of terrorism. The other defines Islam in terms of a crusade against godless Western values. So we have jihad by B52 pitted against jihad by terror – an unholy war. Neither side offers any future beyond the destruction of the other. They're building a new dividing wall right round the world and the world is crying out for someone to start pulling it down before the concrete sets.'

At that point I'd pitched the obvious question:

'And you think that publicising an execution by a group of terrorists sick enough to video it is going to shock people into pulling down this wall?'

He leaned forward, his eyes bright, speaking as though his life depended on his ability to convince me there and then, in front of the camera, in that shabby room.

'He was a man who refused to accept the wall. He went about saying things which threatened to subvert it on both sides. He made enemies left and right. The holy warriors on both sides wanted to get rid of him, out of fear, out of blindness. But he had vision.'

He started stabbing his finger at his forehead, smiling at me.

'I was a holy warrior, I was afraid, I was blind. I … '

At that point, there was a loud crack on the soundtrack. I pressed the stop button.

'And that's as far as we got,' I said. 'You know what happened next.'

'We know what we read in the papers,' said Sue. 'Tell us more.'

I was almost tired of the story but I forced myself into the now familiar narrative. I had to tell Sue and John if I were to ask their advice about the letter.

The video just turned up one day at the reception desk, addressed to me, with a mobile phone number, nothing else. We had it checked of course. It might have been a bomb. I ran it through then showed it to my producer. 'Call that mobile,' she said, and I did.

A man's voice said: 'You're making a programme about terrorism.' a statement, not a question.

'How do you know?'

'Never mind. We need to meet'

I took a taxi. I didn't think I was followed; looking back, I'm not so sure. The man opened the door, let me in cautiously, led me to a back room. We sat on shabby chairs. The window was grey with dirt; I noticed the neglected back garden, the broken shed at the end of it. The brightest thing in the room was the man I'd come to see. He looked at me with eyes shining, as though they were transparent to a light from behind.

A woman came in, older and sad. Her face looked familiar. I couldn't place it.

'Coffee?' she asked.

'Please.'

She left.

'I want you to interview me,' said the man, 'for your programme.'

'Did you make that video?' I asked.

'No, but it's important. I want you to interview me because I know what that video means.'

'Were you there; were you involved in that killing?'

'No. I wasn't there but if I had been I'd have gone along with it.'

'So you're a member of the group that did it; a terrorist?'

'I used to believe in principled use of violence for the greater good. '

'That's terrorist talk,' I said.

'Now I've changed, or rather been changed, by seeing that video, by seeing that death.'

'So you're a reformed terrorist?'

'In a way, yes. And as a result,' the man went on, staring hard at me, speaking slowly for effect, 'my life is now in danger.'

'In danger?'

'Let's say my former employers have a contract out for me.'

While I was weighing that, I asked: 'Tell me, how do you know about the programme?'

'We have friends – contacts.'

At once I was on edge, alarmed. Who were 'we'? Was there a contract out for me, or a time bomb ticking away in the studios? Should I call the police at once, have this man arrested? Instinct said 'yes'. My nose for a good story said 'no'; at least 'not yet'. I steadied myself.

The woman came with the coffee then went again. I was still puzzled by her face.

'Why did you send me that video? Why do you want to talk to me?'

'I've told you,' said the man, sounding irritated. 'I want to tell you what that video means.'

'I can see what it means,' I said. 'It means there are sick and nasty people at large. And they need to be caught.'

'It means a lot more than that. I know it does! You've watched it, yes?'

'Yes. '

'But have you seen it; understood it?' He was stabbing his finger at me. 'Don't look at the people who did the killing. Look at the man they killed!'

'He was innocent?'

'He was more than innocent!' The man leaned forward, thumping the table. 'He held the key to the future! He holds it still. You see, since September 11th… '

'I don't understand,' I interrupted. This man's enthusiasm was casting doubt on his value to me. 'First you say you went along with the killing of this man and now you say he holds the key to the future.'

'Yes! And I want to explain why he… ' He was stabbing me with his finger again.

'Wait!' I said firmly. 'I don't want to know about the man, not now anyway. I accept he was innocent. Terrorism makes all its victims innocent. I'm making a programme about the operation of terrorist groups. If you know something about the group that executed this man and videoed the execution, then of course I'm interested. But you've got to give me something solid to take back to my producer.'

The man leaned back, a wide disarming smile spread over his face.

'I know something about all that – from the inside!' He opened the palms of his hands to me. 'I can help you.'

'You can begin by telling me about yourself.'

He did. He said his name was Paul. Then he went on. When he had finished, I said, 'You realise, don't you, that if we interview you – if we do, then that interview would be evidence for the police. We can't possibly withhold any information about terrorist activity, however circumstantial.'

'I know. I accept that; but one step at a time,' he said, wagging a finger at me and smiling brightly, 'Interview first… please? OK?'

I felt I had a story for the producer now and began to consider the room, thinking about lighting, and camera angles.

The woman returned, asking if we wanted more coffee. Again I looked at her face. And then I realised where I'd seen her before.

After she'd left the room, I said to Paul: 'She's the woman crying in that video, isn't she? Who is she?'

'She's the mother,' said Paul.

'Mother?'

'The mother of the man they killed.'

The next day I returned with Peter, the cameraman, and crew. The mother opened the door. I spoke with her but she was reticent; she didn't want to talk to camera. I wasn't going to press her but I scribbled down what she said. Then we started interviewing Paul.

We'd nearly finished; another couple of questions, another five minutes and I'd have done. Then it happened – two masked men in the garden – been hiding in the shed – gunshots – shattered glass – Peter reeling – blood down his chest – the image of the man in the video flashing across my mind – Paul on the floor – the pain in my hand – more blood, my blood – then silence; and Paul crawling across the floor trying to lift Peter; Paul crying with the bleeding cameraman in his arms. The mother stood weeping at the door. I called the ambulance, the police.

The camera was damaged; we lost half the footage.

Paul's in custody, now. The police and security guys are still questioning him and going through that video, over and over. Of course they wanted to talk to me and I certainly wanted to talk to them. Hard-bitten I may be, but I do have some integrity. That was my interview and I don't want it manipulated just to engineer a conviction.

Peter died in hospital. At the funeral I learned why Paul cried over him on the floor. Peter's wife told me. Peter was Paul's insider, a member of the network, The Way, as they call themselves. It was Peter who told Paul about the programme; left the video at reception.

'But I still don't understand,' said Sue, 'about the video and the interview. They don't connect.'

'I'm not sure myself,' I said, 'and that's what I wanted to talk to you about. You see I had this letter from Paul today.' I took it from my pocket and gave it to them. 'See what you think.'

> Since September 11th, as I told you, the world has been closing the door against a better future, closing the door on hope. Now here's a paradox! In that crucifixion, the world finally slammed the door on the future, and simultaneously God forced it open again! When you interviewed me you only wanted to talk about the door closing, about the terrorists. I wanted to talk about the door opening, about the man the terrorists killed. We in The Way have found that open door, found the vision. We live in hope now! But it's dangerous. Peter is dead. My life is in jeopardy for what I was and for what I am. You think my imagination runs away with me; that I am mad? I cannot come to see you. Please come and see me.

'Half of me wants to,' I said. 'He's intriguing, persuasive. The other half's afraid of that open door. I may be in more trouble than I know already. What should I do?'

Neither John nor Sue would be drawn.

'We don't really know anything about the man they crucified, do we?'

'I did meet his mother,' I said.

'And you haven't told us what she said.'

'She said she was sure her son's spirit would live for ever; not despite his death, but because of it.'

We sat silent for a while. Then together we drank a little more of that excellent red wine.

The axis of evil

In his state of the union address on January 29th 2002, President Bush described Iraq, Iran and North Korea as members of 'an axis of evil'. In the same month there was much news about the collapse of the apparently rich and prosperous American multinational corporation Enron. Thousands lost their jobs and investments in Enron and there were allegations of corrupt accounting practice.

At last they reached the front of the queue. They had been inching forward all morning, under a low grey sky. Now the young couple were at the entrance to the tent. They stood in front of the table.

The woman turned to her husband. 'Do you really think we should?' she asked.

'Yes, my love.' The husband took her hand. 'It is for the best. You can see; everyone thinks so.'

The man sitting behind the table smiled at them.

'You're right,' he said. 'You're investing in your own future.' The wife noticed the gold ring in his ear. She was glad her husband didn't wear an earring. But it hardly mattered now.

Gently the couple placed their gold jewellery on the table – her necklace, his bracelet.

'And your rings?' asked the man.

'Must we?'

'The more you put in now, the more you'll gain later,' said the man.

So, gently, each removed the other's wedding ring, and placed it on the table. They watched as the man dropped their jewellery into the open sack, heard the chink as their precious belongings joined the communal stock. And the wife wondered whether the man would remember to put his own earring in the sack before he tied it.

They turned and left the tent. They did not look at the remaining faces at the end of the queue. Instead they looked up towards the mountain, its majestic height still enveloped in cloud as it had been for many days. It was this cloud, and what it seemed to portend, that had caused uncertainty among the people, uncertainty about their future, about their given destiny. The obscurity above their heads, day and night, seemed to be telling them that it was time now to place a golden deposit on a new future of their own choosing.

Meanwhile, up on the mountain, Moses had his own perspective. He was preparing his state of the nation speech. He sat at the table, pen in hand, with a small pile of plain paper in front of him. So far he had written just one word.

'What are you thinking of saying?' asked God.

God was sitting in his armchair at the other end of the room in the mountain retreat. There the window provided a panoramic view of the valley below – on a clear day, that is. Now God could see nothing below, because of the cloud.

God put the question another way. 'What have you written so far?'

'Amalekites,' replied Moses.

The Amalekites were a vicious dangerous tribe. Their surprise attack had been beaten off only with difficulty. And God had told Moses they would be a threat for a long time to come. It would take generations to vanquish them. And, Moses reflected, it was not just the Amalekites. There were Caananites, Jebusites, Hittites, Perrizites – a great axis of evil ranged against the people. Moses liked the phrase 'axis of evil', so he wrote it down. He hoped God would like it too. Moses was not good with words. He had told God so at the beginning but God had said that that was no bar to leadership and told him to appoint his brother Aaron as spokesperson and deputy. Since then, Moses felt, his communication skills had improved. He hoped God thought so too, though God never commented. And God said nothing now. He was staring intently though the window, as though his eyes were penetrating the cloud.

Moses found it hard to make God out. Sometimes he seemed like an experienced friend who had already been where Moses was going, who knew what was round the corner. At other times God seemed to be discovering what it was like to be God on the move, just as Moses was learning to be the leader of an itinerant, expectant, often truculent people.

Amalekites apart, Moses thought, things were going reasonably well at the moment. Earlier problems – lack of food and water – had been overcome. Delegating to Aaron worked well now, so Moses could spend more time at the mountain retreat with God, mapping out the future. A deposit of gold had been found, and people were panning in the stream that flowed down the mountain. Increasingly women wore gold ornaments, and some men too. Moses disliked jewellery for men; he especially disliked Aaron's earring. It set a bad example. Moses also feared that wealth would lead to greed. He was glad about God's ruling against golden idols; it was a wise preventive measure. Moses had seen enough idolatry in Egypt and he knew what that could do to people. The big problem was undoubtedly the Amalekites and the axis of evil. That must be the theme of his speech. And, as if to endorse his conclusion, a shaft of sunlight suddenly illuminated the word in front of him.

Moses looked up. 'The axis of evil,' he said brightly. 'What do you think?'

God was standing at the window now, looking down to the valley, his face almost pressed against the glass.

'I think you had better come here,' said God. His voice was hard, controlled.

Moses went to the window. He looked. The cloud had cleared. He could see a crowd, gathering round a bright object, like ants around an insect corpse. Its shape was obscured by its reflected light. It shone golden.

'What is it?' asked Moses.

God exploded. 'I knew it! I knew it!' he shouted, banging his fist against the glass. The glass broke. God cut his hand. The blood began to flow. Moses grabbed a cloth from the table and wrapped it round God's hand. God noticed neither wound nor dressing. He sank into the chair, threw his head back, closed his eyes, then held his wounded hand with the uninjured one. His chest heaved. He seemed to struggle for breath.

Moses, taken aback by this outburst, stood speechless, his back to the window.

God opened his eyes and stared angrily at Moses.

'Who set them free?' he said, raising his voice. 'I did. Who provided food and water? I did! Who has protected them day and night? I have.

Who has given them something to hope for, something to live for? I have! I have! And why? Why?' God paused, then shouted, 'Because I love them! That's why!' He paused again. 'Take them away! Take them away!'

And with that God bent forward, his head almost on his knees.

Moses stood and stared at God. This was no Olympian fury. This was anger as of a loving husband who finds his wife unfaithful, who hurls her photograph at the wall, and then breaks down in tears. God was crying now.

'Take them away,' came though the sobs. 'Take them away!'

Then Moses, struggling for words, said something wholly inappropriate, which he at once regretted.

'What would the Egyptians say... that, that you set them free and then abandoned them?'

'You can lead them,' said God, still bent.

'But I am not god. We need you.'

'You lead them,' repeated God. Then, lifting his head, he looked tearfully at Moses. 'Go. Look after them. Take them.'

Awkwardly Moses turned and looked out of the window. The crowd had grown and was now solidified around the golden object. And a man stood in the middle. Moses looked at the man intently, narrowing his eyes to focus. There was no doubt. It was his brother.

'My God,' said Moses quietly; then again shouting, in rising anger, 'My God!'

'Now you know how I feel,' said God steadily. He had risen and was standing beside Moses. 'You had better go.'

God watched Moses as he made his way down the mountain, stepping between the boulders, following the course of the stream. Then he looked down into the valley. A ring of fire now burned round the golden idol, the smoke rising in the clear air.

Well before he reached the crowd, Moses heard the chanting.

'Enron, Enron, Enron, Enron.'

Then he saw the people circling slowly round the fire, round the idol, hands held high, palms upwards.

'Enron, Enron, Enron, Enron.'

Moses, striding, pushing, forced his way to the centre of the crowd. People made way, fell silent. From where they were standing, the young couple watched as Moses confronted Aaron. Moses' voice they heard clearly. What Aaron said they could only gather from Moses' tirade.

'What do you mean, "You had to do it"… "The people wanted it" … You're supposed to be a leader!… "You weren't around."? Where do you think I was? On vacation?… "Amalekites"? Do you think dancing round that thing is going to protect you from the Amalekites?… "Security" If you want security, go back to Egypt and be a slave again!'

Moses turned to the people.

'Do you want to go back to Egypt, to feel the whip on your back in the noonday sun? Do you?'

There was a shaking of heads, there were downcast eyes, there was silence.

'Well you don't need to go back. You have made slaves of yourselves here, today; slaves to your wealth, slaves to your greed.'

Moses stepped forward. He stood now right in front of the golden calf. Then at some risk to himself, he reached over the fire, grasped the idol and hurled it down into the flames.

There was silence, whether of acquiescence or resentment, Moses was uncertain.

God watched. He was sitting outside the retreat now, beside the stream. Carefully he removed the blood-soaked cloth from his hand. The wound was open. God bathed it; his blood coloured the clear water, and flowed on down. God wondered how long the wound would take to heal; as long, he thought, as it would take him to fulfil his commitment to bring the people to the Promised Land. And this, he knew, would not be the last love in anger wound on the way, the last idol to be erected and then cast down. The axis of evil threatened the people he loved, from within as well as without.

The young couple walked home to their tent. They said little. They were unsure of what they had lost and gained that day. They stopped by the stream, knelt down at the waterside and gently washed each other's hands and faces.

Slaying the dragon

On February 13th 2002, President Bush, speaking of Iraq, said that while he 'looked forward to working with the world' to bring pressure to bear on Saddam Hussein, 'America reserves the right to confront Saddam' if he fails to abandon the development of weapons of mass destruction. During February there was much press speculation about the prospect of a US attack on Iraq later in the year, and about the wisdom of such an attack.

The king stood on top of the highest mountain in his kingdom. His was a big kingdom, and he was a big king, to match his kingdom. He felt bigger than usual on top of the mountain. He could see a long way in all directions and, seeing, he felt in control.

He could look west across the rolling countryside of his own realm. He enjoyed doing that. He liked looking down on the bright and prosperous farmland, towards the city sparkling in the sun and his palace rising above it.

He liked looking north and south towards the neighbouring kingdoms, not so big, so bright, so prosperous as his. That made him feel good, as did the fact that the neighbouring kings acknowledged him as the biggest king, and welcomed the trade and protection he offered. The big king felt in some vague way responsible for them, as for his own kingdom.

All this was important to the big king, because behind his size and power hid a weakness, which repeatedly troubled him. Inside was a little voice crying out for reassurance, usually when the king was alone, at night in the dark, in his dreams. However many times his courtiers praised his wise judgement, however many times the people cheered when he appeared in the streets, however many times the neighbouring kings sought his advice, he never felt quite sure of himself. What, asked the insistent voice inside, what did they really think; what did they really say behind his back?

The king had got himself into a state of mind now in which he felt he needed to do something decisive, something successful beyond question, something which would secure his place in history.

That is why he had come to the mountaintop. And that is why he looked not west, or north or south, but east, at the deep dark forest. He could see a plume of smoke, oily black smoke, rising in the distance through the trees. There, he knew, was the great thing he had to do. He must kill the dragon; or rather, get his soldiers to kill the dragon.

The dragon was, there could be no doubt about it, evil and a menace. The eastern forest would always be beyond civilization, beyond the big king's influence, as long as the dragon inhabited it, breathing daily fire and smoke. The poisonous oily smoke sometimes drifted over the great kingdom. It settled on growing vegetables; it made people cough; some coughed so much that they died. The forest creatures, of course, suffered very badly. Word was that many died each year from dragon smoke. And they, poor things, were powerless against the dragon.

The king had already persuaded his neighbours to join him in sending a very strongly worded letter to the dragon telling it to exhale its poisonous smoke only when the wind was blowing the other way, towards Nowhere. (This would not of course have helped the forest creatures much.) The dragon snorted and burned the letter.

Then the king sent spies into the forest. They wore masks to try and protect themselves from the oily smoke. They came back and reported that the dragon was constructing a great war machine. From the photographs, experts concluded that it was probably capable of hurling dragon-fired tree trunks over great distances, carrying poisonous smoke possibly as far as the big king's city. This meant that the big kingdom was in great danger.

The big king knew he had to act. This was his hour. But he was not foolhardy. He wanted to do the right thing, as a big king should. Not altogether trusting either his courtiers or the neighbouring kings, he decided privately to seek the advice of the Wandering Wise Man. He had been told that the Wise Man was wandering on the high mountain and the king had climbed to talk to him.

'Do not go to war without first counting the cost,' said the Wandering Wise Man.

In bed that night the king lay thinking, trying to count the cost. He had strong soldiers – big, nearly as big as himself – plenty of them, heavily armed with long spears. Mind you, he thought, spears are not quite so effective in thick forest. The trees tend to get in the way. Nonetheless, military power was not a problem. Victory could almost be guaranteed.

Then there were the forest creatures. They suffered from the dragon already and they would suffer more in a war. But if the war killed the dragon, then they would be free. Furthermore, if he didn't kill the dragon and the dragon started hurling his burning tree trunks, innocent people in his own kingdom would be killed and people would blame him for not protecting them. The king shuddered at the thought of such criticism.

Then there were his neighbours. They were not as strong as he. They might be hesitant about fighting the dragon, fearing tree trunks launched against their own kingdoms in retaliation. But they depended on the big king's protection. They might raise objections but victory would appease them, no doubt.

And then above all there was the prospect of a stunning victory against the heart of evil resident in the dark forest and the big king's name bannered in large heroic letters across the world. His place in history would be secure, unassailable – the king of peace. That settled the matter. Altogether, the king concluded, this would be a just war. Then he closed his eyes, and slept a dreamless sleep. Next morning he called his commander and ordered preparations for battle.

The war against the dragon was of course a success. The dragon was slain and buried in a huge hole in the middle of the forest. The king decreed a two-day holiday to commemorate the victory. But the costs were higher than the king had hoped. Some brave soldiers were incinerated, and amid the celebrations their families mourned. Many forest creatures were killed – some burned alive by the dragon, some severed by soldiers' spears that went astray among the trees (a higher percentage of mis-hits than army experts had predicted). And many forest creatures, driven from their homes, sought refuge in neighbouring kingdoms and began eating their way through carefully cultivated vegetables.

A few days after the battle, the king climbed the hill again, to survey his victory. He studied the forest. It was deeply scarred; great areas of trees destroyed, some cut down by his own soldiers, some turned to ashes by dragon fire. The king could see one fire still smouldering – or was it smouldering? The king blinked and strained his eyes. The smoke was oily black. Its source seemed to be moving, as though the residual fire were itself on the move. The king stared and stared, first interested, then puzzled and then suddenly horrified. Could it be – appalling thought – could it be that another dragon had entered the forest from Nowhere?

Someone tapped him on the shoulder. The king froze. He knew who it was.

'Well,' said a voice behind him, gently and with no animosity or irony, 'did you count the cost correctly?'

The king turned round. He said nothing, looked the Wandering Wise Man in the face, then looked down at his own big boots.

'Few kings ever do,' said the Wise Man. 'It's sad, isn't it? However well intentioned, kings always diminish themselves when they go to war. I've often thought this world needs a new kind of kingship.'

That night the big king did not sleep well. In fact he had a terrible dream. He dreamt that he was lying on a bed that was getting bigger and bigger. The commander of his army stood beside the bed, looking huge, as big as the bed. But suddenly the king realised; neither bed nor commander were larger than life. He, the king, had shrunk. He woke in a sweat, shaking. He slept no more that night. And in the morning he instructed that his appointments for the day be cancelled. He would meet the families of soldiers killed in the dragon war on another occasion.

Amos and daughter

On March 29th 2002 (Good Friday) at the end of a week of escalating violence between Israelis and Palestinians, including several suicide bombings, a Palestinian schoolgirl, Ayat Akhras, blew herself up outside a shop in Jerusalem. She killed two Israeli civilians as well as herself. The al-Aqsa Martyrs Brigade provided her with the explosives to strap to her body.

Amos sat outside the street café, facing the square. A handful of people were resting on the stone steps at its centre, but not many, for the summer sun was intense. The noon heat was oppressive; so were the traffic fumes; so were the armed soldiers, at every street corner round the square and the police patrolling the pavements with expressionless faces. Amos, the countryman, was always uncomfortable in the city. He felt an alien. His heart was, and always would be, in his hillside village above the river.

He ordered a coffee, and wondered how to find Leila. She had disappeared. He wondered what he would say to her, his much loved daughter, if and when he found her. They had been so close, in the village, during the war. Together, they had sheltered in their cellar from shells; had knelt in the street outside the house beside his wife, Leila's mother, as she lay dying from a sniper's bullet. They had shared the fear, shared the grief.

Together they had abandoned their home, when the enemy, after days of street fighting, finally overwhelmed the shattered village. They had gone to what seemed like the comparative safety of his brother's house in the capital. But even there the shelling pursued them.

The fighting eventually stopped. International diplomats managed to broker a crude and unstable ceasefire between what they patronizingly called 'the warring factions'. Aid was promised. The enemy, for the most part victorious, had been persuaded to exchange Amos's village for gains elsewhere and Amos wanted to go home. But Leila said she would not go with him. At first Amos understood. The wounds of her teenage grief were still bleeding. But then she had begun to withdraw from him, as though she blamed him somehow for her mother's death.

Amos had tried gently, perhaps ineptly, to explain to her something he only half understood himself – the madness of war, the gut instinct to hate because you are hated, the fear that made even him, her father, take a gun, pull the trigger and lust for blood. And above all, he spoke of his duty to protect his loved ones, his home, his ancestral land. But Leila insisted that it was a war about nothing. She wept for her mother, and raged at her father for the ethnic madness of his generation, for blighting her future with futility. Then she withdrew into herself, stayed in bed during the day, stayed awake at night, spent a lot of time out of the apartment, avoided her father whenever she could, and turned away when he tried to kiss her.

And so Amos had returned alone to the village, to their empty house, with its bullet-pitted walls, its half broken, red-tiled roof, its damp rooms looted of family belongings. Amos hadn't had the heart to walk round his orchard. He knew without looking that the fruit trees, his livelihood, would be ruined. The evening had been warm and sunny. Amos had sat on his doorstep, crying as he remembered Leila helping with the fruit picking, Leila the affectionate pre-war child, a ribbon in her waving hair. Later he'd picked a few wild flowers and taken them to his wife's neglected grave. He had sat there, crying again, wondering at the injustice that had inflicted this grief upon him. He had sat looking down on the river, until its slow waters turned grey and then black in the dusk.

The waiter brought the coffee. Amos drank, still wondering how he, a villager, should find his daughter in the complex city. His street-wise brother had tried and failed.

A large, black saloon with police motorcycle escort glided round the square. A small crowd on the other side of the square shouted something as the big car passed. Amos watched as the snorting motorbikes shepherded it down the avenue leading off the square towards the big new hotel.

'That's where the aid money goes,' said Amos to the waiter, pointing to the car and the hotel. The waiter shrugged, and went inside.

Amos had little money. The local fruit-processing factory, once the seasonal lifeline for local farmers, had been shelled. Its gates were padlocked. There was no money to reopen it. There was talk of new export markets for farmers, of credit, but so far it was talk only. Amos, like other villagers, felt himself imprisoned and impotent between an irrecoverable past and a doubtful future. Without his wife to give value to his past or his daughter to give shape to his future, Amos felt his love poised directionless, pent up in a solitary no man's land.

Another limousine made its way to the hotel. A tank crawled round the corner and settled menacingly across the square. The little crowd responded with a rythmic chanting. A police van burst out of a side road; officers in riot gear leapt out. There was a scuffle. The chanting stopped. The police stood shoulder to shoulder, facing the crowd, their backs to Amos.

The waiter reappeared.

'More coffee?'

'What's going on? asked Amos.

'International conference,' said the waiter.

'What about?'

'Stabilization,' said the waiter.

'Stabilization?'

The waiter shrugged, and went inside again.

Down a side street, away from the square, was another café. In a back room, well out of sight of any passing police officer, sat two young people – a man and a girl, he perhaps in his twenties, she still in her teens. They had finished their coffee. They spoke in whispers, intimately, intensely, like lovers on edge. But they were not lovers. The young man was calm, looking steadily at the girl as he spoke, his hands hidden beneath the table. The girl was smoking, inhaling deeply. At first she calmly returned the man's gaze, as though absorbing information from his eyes rather than his mouth. Then suddenly she was nervous, stubbed a half-smoked cigarette, lit another, repeatedly brushed her lank dyed hair out of her eyes. She held a brown envelope. She turned it over and over in her hand.

From under the table the man produced a face mask painted like a death's head. He gave it to her. He also gave her a small black bag. The

girl at once concealed the bag in her anorak. She gave the man the
envelope; then left the table, went to the toilet. The man pocketed the
envelope, paid for the coffee, and waited. It was several minutes before
the girl returned. Though the day was dry and hot, she was wearing the
anorak. Outside the café they parted without a word. She walked
towards the square, carrying the mask. The man went the opposite way.

Amos finished his coffee, paid for it and walked slowly round the
square. A third limousine passed, escorted like the others and greeted
by abusive shouts from the crowd. Amos thought he saw a stone
thrown. 'If these men in black cars are here to help us,' he thought to
himself, 'why do they make such a show of protecting themselves from
us?' He looked at the branded designer goods in the shop windows.
'You could afford these,' he thought, 'if you owned a big black car.' No
one in his village had that sort of money to spend. 'It's an unbalanced
world,' said Amos, 'an unjust one.'

He found himself walking towards the demonstrators. Now he
could see through the gaps in the police cordon. He could see death
masks in the crowd. Soldiers and police officers eyed him, a shabby,
solitary middle-aged man, but they did not move. Amos was near the
crowd now. Suddenly he felt uneasy, decided to turn back. He
hesitated, as some movement in the crowd caught his eye. Someone
had broken through the police cordon, was running fast straight
towards him – a figure in a mask and an anorak. There was a gunshot.
The figure stumbled, got up, came on, limping now. Amos stood
frozen. But the masked figure never reached him, for the police
pounced on their prey. They grabbed her, truncheoned her, dragged
her to the police van and virtually threw her into the back, leapt in after
her and slammed the van door shut.

The van swung round and raced out of the square, down the side
street. Amos stood shaking from head to foot, for, instantly, he had
known who the masked figure was.

Seconds later there was a loud explosion from the side street. The
police van was blown apart. All its occupants were of course killed
outright; so were ten passers by. Several more lay seriously injured in
pools of blood on the pavement. Others ran screaming into the square.

Later that day Amos stood by the window in his brother's tower block
apartment. He looked absently at the block opposite, once bustling

with families, now a silent hollow monument to shelling. Children played in the rubble.

He held the brown envelope which had been pushed under the door sometime earlier in the day. There was a message on the back. He had not noticed it before. It simply said 'Call… ' and there was a mobile phone number. The handwriting on the envelope was not Leila's, but the letter was hers.

> Dear Father,
> I know you are looking for me, but you will not find me. For by the time you read this I will have answered God's call. You told me you fought to avoid sacrifice. You were wrong to do so. This is a holy war in which ultimate victory comes only through sacrifice. I am making that sacrifice; today I join the noble army of martyrs. God is great! I love you. Go home now. I will pray for you. Please put flowers on my mother's grave.
> Your daughter, Leila.

Amos wept.

It was bad enough to lose a daughter, horrific to lose her in this way, with her last words to him in a letter so chilling, so impersonal. And what malign fate, he wondered though his tears, arranged that he, searching for her, should witness her self-destruction, without a word spoken? When she ran towards him what had she wanted to say? Would they have embraced? Could he have changed her mind, released her from whatever spell she was under? Had he lost his daughter through his own lack of understanding or had she been stolen away from him by the devils who had masked her? Could he there, in the square, in front of the police, have saved his daughter?

Amos tortured himself over all this, sitting with his brother far into the night. Sleep came to him at last, but not before he had agreed to his brother's suggestion, that he call the phone number on the envelope.

The next day, the young man who had steeled the daughter for self-sacrifice now faced her broken-hearted father across the same café table. The young man offered coffee. Amos shook his head. The only word he could say was 'Why?'

The young man spoke the same strange language Amos had read in Leila's letter. It was as though he were fitting together a familiar jigsaw of phrases already pre-loaded in his brain. He spoke quickly.

'God is great! This is a holy war. The enemy within is imposed on us by the greater enemy without. The enemy within is the government. They govern in the interests of those who put them there. Those who put them there are those who defeated us in the war, those who raped our women, took our land, occupied our villages, made our people homeless, and oppress us daily.'

Amos interrupted. 'Where did you meet my daughter?'

'Here, in this café. God be praised! Hers is a glorious victory.'

'My daughter killed herself yesterday,' said Amos. 'She was just eighteen years old.'

'She is with the saints in glory. She saw the truth. She saw that our resistance to the enemy was futile so long as we fought as they fought; and they had weapons and money, which we have not. They were armed by the enemy without. We were defeated because our people were not prepared to sacrifice themselves to achieve victory over evil. '

Amos thought of his beloved wife slumped against the wall of their house, in a pool of blood. He remembered Leila kneeling at her side, screaming.

'My daughter loved life,' said Amos.

'She loved the life of paradise. She knew that ultimate victory comes through the sacrifice of oneself. God be praised! God is just!'

'She did not want to die! She did not!'

Amos felt the rising distress in his own voice; but the young man did not sense it. He continued.

'The war is not over. Why has the enemy without arranged a conference in this city? They speak of "stabilization". They will give more money to our government, for more weapons, more troops, more police, more repression, more denial of our rights. They are not concerned about us as people; they are worried by us as a problem. They are not concerned about families who have lost their homes, about children in refugee camps. But they are worried about what they call terrorism. Homeless children do not threaten the enemy without. But terrorism does. Our enemies within and without are scared of those prepared to sacrifice their lives for justice. That is why we must continue this holy war.'

'And you will sacrifice your life? asked Amos bitterly. 'You will be the next suicide bomber?'

'My time is not yet. It will come. The end time is approaching. Martyrdom is victory. God be praised!'

'Tell me what did my daughter say to you – her last words.'

'She said, "Today I will be in paradise. I will pray for you there."'

Amos could stand no more. Abruptly he got up and made for the door. There he turned and faced the man, still sitting.

'Liar!' he shouted with tears in his eyes. 'Liar! Liar! Murderer!'

In a pathetic gesture, he seized a coffee cup from the counter, hurled it at the young man, and then ran down the street towards the square. The square was quiet. Amos sat on the stone steps a long time, his head buried in his hands.

Months later he sat similarly beside the grave, which was now, for him, his daughter's as well as his wife's. Winter had come; rain had fallen for days. The river was fast and swollen. Amos had been thinking, for weeks now, thinking his own thoughts, not implanted ones – thoughts born of his own bitter experience.

Leila's suicide, he was sure, was an act of despair. It was a cry for help from a girl already convinced no help will come. Sometimes he almost comforted himself with the thought that she at least died believing her sacrifice was worthwhile. But mostly he cursed the young man with his perverse dogma for persuading Leila, the girl who loved life, that she could ennoble her despair by ending her own and other innocent lives. He cursed the causes of her despair, which was his despair also. He cursed the war, the poverty, the death of hope. He cursed injustice. With a mighty gesture, he imagined himself sweeping it off the face of the earth.

Amos looked at the swollen river. It reflected his thoughts.

'Let justice roll down like waters, and righteousness like an ever flowing stream!'

'That's what I want to say!' shouted Amos out loud, standing up. 'Give me a big black car, and I'll drive from conference to stabilization conference. Justice is the word from the country to the cities. God is great!'

The Passover Massacre

On March 28th 2002, at the start of the Passover
festival, a Palestinian suicide bomber killed 15 people
and injured one hundred in a hotel in Natanya. Hamas
claimed responsibility. The Israeli government called
this the Passover Massacre. On the same day the Arab
Summit agreed on a peace plan put forward by Saudi
Arabia. Saudi Crown Prince Abdullah said, 'We believe
in peace based on justice and equity. Only within the
context of true peace can normal relations flourish
between the people of the region.'

The dinner was finished. The great King of Arabia watched as the last
of the slave girls removed the remaining food. Her face was downcast,
her eyes lowered, as she approached the royal presence. She looked
neither left nor right but only at the silver dish containing the uneaten
roast lamb. Gracefully she bent, lifted the dish from the table,
straightened her body then walked backwards, the customary ten
paces, paused, turned, and disappeared through the curtains. Only the
wine remained on the low table and the two kings were alone.

Pharaoh turned to his guest. 'You would like more wine?'

The King of Arabia nodded with a smile and held out his goblet.
Pharaoh poured.

'May I ask you something?' said the king.

Now Pharaoh nodded.

That slave girl,' began the king. 'She's beautiful. She looked... '

Pharaoh cut in.

'Do not be deceived by looks,' he said. With a gesture towards the
curtain, Pharaoh lowered his voice, to a whisper. 'I trust none of them.
The palace guard are under orders to watch them day and night,
especially at night. The whole of Egypt is on alert.'

'How has this come about?'

Pharaoh explained. The slaves, or at least malcontents among them who claimed to be spokesmen, were agitating. They claimed to want freedom. He had granted an audience to their leaders. They made deceptively reasonable suggestions.

'They talk about their right to be free for a while to worship their god in the desert. I am not deceived by that; not after their acts of sabotage.'

Pharaoh described the river pollution, the damage to crops and other ills, which could be attributed, he claimed, to subversive slaves.

'So what will you do?' asked his guest.

'I will eradicate the agitators among them. They are sowing seeds of terror across the land. My soldiers are searching for them from house to house, with orders to kill. The slaves will stay. They are essential to our economy. They will be subject to stricter controls.'

Pharaoh stood up, and raising his voice said: 'I have an eternal duty. It is to protect my people, the prosperity of my kingdom, the glory of this house.' He intoned this as though it were the creed befitting a god king; which is what he, and his people, believed him to be.

His guest was respectfully silent but he was thinking about the beautiful and demure girl with the downcast eyes, unable to see beyond lifetime subservience.

'Might I make a suggestion?' asked the King of Arabia.

Pharaoh sat down again, nodded, put his finger to his lips. The king lowered his voice, inclining his head towards Pharaoh.

'Had you considered,' whispered the king slowly, carefully, 'considered – granting them, the trustworthy ones that is, a measure of self determination… '

Pharaoh began to shake his head, vigorously.

'Within conditions, naturally,' said the king quickly. 'But limited concessions could – how shall I put it – disarm the agitators, the terrorists. Yes?'

'No,' whispered Pharaoh emphatically. 'That would be interpreted as weakness, by my people as well as by the slaves. It would only encourage their malcontents to press for more.'

The king began another line of argument. 'You say they are asking for the right to worship… '

'They have no rights!' said Pharaoh. 'They are property.'

As Pharaoh`s guest, the King of Arabia thought he should not press the matter further. The conversation turned to other things – the harvest, the fine temple that Pharaoh had just completed, and the excellence of the wine. But the king kept thinking of the slave girl, and by the end of the evening in his imagination he had adopted her as the daughter he had always wanted. He could see her adorning his palace, dressed in a royal robe of silk, embroidered with golden thread.

Time came to retire for the night. The king, with the girl still on his mind, could not help returning to the subject of the slaves, offering to draft a plan himself to pacify the land, which would both guarantee some self-determination to the slaves, and security to the Egyptians.

If Pharaoh was irritated by this, he concealed his feelings. He smiled a non-committal smile and assured his esteemed guest that he, Pharaoh, considered it a pleasure to entertain him, and that there would be two armed guards alert outside his bedchamber all night. His guest's security was his greatest concern, and was guaranteed.

That night the slaves throughout the land rose up and perpetrated a massive terrorist attack. It was well coordinated, and was certainly carried out with confidence that it would achieve the desired result.

The firstborn son in every Egyptian family was executed, swiftly, silently, in the dark. Vigilant palace guards failed to save Pharaoh's oldest son and by dawn the ruler of Egypt was a broken man. The previous night, with the confidence of semi-divinity, he had told his royal guest that freedom for slaves was unthinkable. Before sunrise he had conceded it. And his guest, the King of Arabia, woke to find that the slaves were already making their way into the desert.

The king thought it tactful to return at once to his own kingdom, and prudent also. Who could say how widespread the consequences of this crisis might be? He expressed his deepest condolences to his host and then rode out through the palace gates, through a crowd of Egyptians come to express their feelings to their Pharaoh.

Their feelings were mixed. Some simply grieved as parents. Some were angry as landowners now without labour. All wanted to know what Pharaoh intended to do.

Pharaoh spent the morning in his innermost room with his closest advisers. By noon he had decided. He sent word to the crowd at the gate. He had instructed the army on horseback to chase the slaves, capture them and bring them back. As the slaves were on foot and unarmed, this should not be a problem. When the slaves had been recovered their leaders would be executed, and the rest returned to their employers. The country, Pharaoh reassured his people, would be normalized

What Pharaoh did not tell the people was that, to avoid further bloodshed, he would grant to slaves who proved themselves trustworthy a limited, very limited, measure of freedom, to worship their god. Now was clearly not the right time to mention this but he was committed enough to the idea to send a swift messenger after the King of Arabia, requesting his help. He reflected that if the measure was a failure, he could always blame it on the interference of a foreign power.

Then he absorbed himself in his personal grief, and waited for news of the army.

The news, when it came, was disastrous. Before the army could reach the slaves they had somehow crossed the Red Sea and the army had found itself engulfed in impassable waters. Many soldiers had drowned.

Pharaoh raged pointlessly at the messenger; dismissed his advisers, and sat alone in his inner room. He, the great god-king, felt utterly defeated in reputation, in policy and in spirit. He prayed for guidance. But his god had nothing helpful to say. His god was too small. Pharaoh realized that he was praying to himself. He thought bitterly that the slave god seemed to have done rather better for the slaves.

The King of Arabia sat still on his horse by the highway, listening to Pharaoh's messenger dismounted beside him. He sent the messenger back with renewed condolences, but no renewal of his offer of help. The king, of course, knew nothing about the destruction of Pharaoh's army. But he knew that the slaves had seen the sun rise on their freedom; that they would accept nothing from Pharaoh now. He thought of the lovely slave girl. She was probably bent over a cooking pot somewhere surrounded by sand. He reproached himself for his covetous dream about her. She would always be better off as a free woman than as an ornamental princess.

The king rode briskly on towards his own land. He feared for the future. 'There will,' he thought, 'be other terrorist massacres, as other oppressed people become desperate, and other innocent people will be killed because other pharaohs wilfully disregard other peace opportunities.'

Perhaps, one day, there might come some ultimate slaughter of the ultimate innocent, as a result of which the world would be ultimately doomed – or, perhaps, ultimately saved but not, he thought, in his time, not in his kingdom.

He suddenly reined in his horse and sat stock still. A sharp question had stabbed his conscience. Would he have the courage to do in his own kingdom what he had advised Pharaoh to do in Egypt?

The great King of Arabia rode on, but more slowly now.

Father Marcus rings the bell

On April 2nd 2002, Israeli troops surrounded the Church of the Nativity in Bethlehem. More than 200 people had taken refuge inside, including priests, Palestinian civilians and gunmen named and wanted by the Israelis as terrorists. The priests failed to persuade the gunmen to leave. Israeli forces shot and killed a few Palestinians outside the church, but did not enter. The stand-off ended early in May. The gunmen in the church were exiled under an agreement brokered by foreign diplomats.

A gloomy morning light shone through the windows of the village church in the valley. The priest had hardly slept. Dispirited and hungry, he celebrated the Mass. The flames of the two altar candles trembled, shivered, as though they shared the chill and the fear of the tiny congregation scattered on the front pews. The mayor sat among them, staring blankly at the stained glass saint in the window behind the altar.

'"The day before He suffered, He took bread… After supper He took the cup…"'

Father Marcus mouthed the words, thinking to himself, 'It's now the third day since these people took refuge here, the third day without food.'

The imprisoned congregation stood up untidily and shuffled forward to receive the sacrament. They were all familiar villagers, except one young man. He was dressed in jeans and a hooded anorak, sitting half hidden until now behind the statuette of Virgin and Child, which protruded from the wall. Father Marcus was certain he had not been in the church when darkness fell the previous evening. Now, suddenly, as the stranger came forward to receive the bread, the priest felt uneasy about him, just as he felt uneasy about the men at the other end of the church, gathered in the recess beneath the bell tower. He counted. There were still four of them, sitting at a rough table, their Kalashnikovs against the wall.

The stranger smiled at Father Marcus as he received the bread. Some in the congregation noticed this, their curiosity tinged with a little hope. Perhaps, it dawned on them, the stranger was a good sign. For if he had been able to get into the church unhindered last night, might they not be able to get out unhindered this morning? Perhaps he had come to help them in some way.

The priest concluded the Mass. He lifted the little crucifix from the altar and held it high.

"May the blessing of Almighty God… "

The gunmen at the back looked at the crucifix. They thought of the self-sacrifice they planned for later. They had thought of little else all night. The other resistance fighters who had survived the soldiers' shelling and the street fighting had retreated to the nearby hills to regroup. But these four had entered the church to prepare for their final mission. Its solid walls and sacred statues would, they thought, give them temporary protection, and perhaps impart a blessing, for their mission was, they believed, holy as well as just.

The involuntary congregation stayed where they were. There was nowhere to go. They felt good reason to hate and shield themselves from the soldiers who had shelled and tanked their way into the village, shot their way from house to house, killing gunmen and unarmed alike. But they were not comfortable with the four men beneath the bell tower. They shared the gunmen's sense of oppressive injustice. They recognized the heroic in them but they also feared the danger of being too close to heroes. They had heard their priest telling them that their guns profaned the church; they had heard the gunmen refuse to leave.

So the weakened villagers stayed, nursing their hunger, at one end of the church. The gunmen, equally hungry but careless of food, contemplated their destiny at the other.

In the aisle between, Father Marcus listened while the mayor quietly questioned the young stranger.

'You are not local,' said the mayor.

'Yes and no,' said the stranger. 'I was born here.'

'Why have you come?' asked the mayor suspiciously.

'To be with my people.'

'Did the soldiers send you in?'

'No.'

'Did they see you come?'

'It was dark.'

Father Marcus thought these answers economical, but he was too tired to interrogate. And a more immediate question concerned him.

'Have you food?' he asked. 'We have been without for three days.'

The stranger's reply, whatever it was, was lost in the crackle of a loudhailer springing to life outside the altar window, the other side of the saint.

'Attention! Attention!' shouted a soldier in an unsaintly voice, distorted by amplification. 'Come out unarmed, and you will be free to return to your homes! I repeat, come out unarmed, and you will be free!'

The message was repeated without variation, at intervals, over the next half hour. Each announcement increased the tension inside the church.

Priest, mayor and people stood together by the altar. The leading gunman joined them. The stranger stood at the edge of the group, listening, saying nothing.

'Don't trust them' said the gunman urgently. Nobody did. But nobody was sure what to do.

The mayor was incensed that the soldiers, having destroyed people's homes, now had the gall, and the power, to give or withhold permission to return to them. He ran the village café. He had food in store. He could distribute it. That would be a mayoral thing to do. But then again the soldiers had probably looted the storeroom by now.

Some villagers felt like risking their lives for food now. Others preferred to endure their hunger in the comparative safety of the church. Some felt solidarity with the gunmen, whose death was near certain if they were left alone in the church.

'Don't trust them' repeated the gunman, insistently. Nobody did.

The voice of the army fell silent. But the soldiers with their tanks waited outside. Their officer told them they were under orders to stay and destroy the little piece of the terrorist infrastructure holed up inside the church. And he had received a further instruction, which he chose to keep to himself for the moment. His men knew that, sooner or later, hunger would force the people out of the church. And if the gunmen did not follow, then they would be free to enter the church and kill them.

Father Marcus was thinking along similar lines, deeply worried about the spilling of blood in his church. 'If that happened,' he thought, 'I would have failed as a priest; unless,' he added after further thought, 'the blood spilt were mine.' As long as the gunmen remained in the church, he decided, he must stay too. If necessary he must be their ultimate human shield. Father Marcus looked towards the crucifix.

'What are you thinking?' asked a voice beside him. It was the young stranger.

'I'm thinking,' said the priest, surprised at his own candour, 'that I am out of my depth. I am just a middle-aged village priest. My seminary training never equipped me for these extremes of pastoral care.'

'Let's talk to our friends at the back of the church,' said the stranger.

'Friends?' Father Marcus was suddenly uneasy again, very uneasy, about the stranger. He sensed crisis.

He followed the stranger to the back of the church where the gunmen sat by the table, their Kalashnikovs still in line, stark against the whitewashed wall. Under the table was a large holdall.

'When are you going to do it then?' asked the stranger.

'Do what?' asked the leading gunman.

'The suicide bombing,' said the stranger, pointing to the holdall.

'How did you know… ?'

'Never mind. I know. When?'

'After dark – tonight. By morning the soldiers, those left alive, will have withdrawn. We will have set these people free to return to their homes.' He looked at Father Marcus. 'Your congregation will have bread tomorrow.'

'And you think to bring peace in this way?' asked the stranger.

'How else can we fight, against a well-organized army with such firepower? It will be a victory – because we sacrifice our lives it will be a victory. There is no victory without sacrifice.'

'If the sacrifice is in a spirit of hatred,' said the stranger, 'it is not a victory, it is a defeat.' And he turned to go back down the aisle.

'Now wait a minute!' shouted one of the gunmen angrily. He got up and made to grab the stranger.

His leader restrained him.

'For God's sake leave him alone! Keep your mind on the mission.'

And he shouted at Father Marcus: 'Keep him out of our way! Is that understood?'

Priest and stranger stood together by the wall, beside the statuette of Virgin and Child.

Father Marcus looked the young man in the face.

'I should have said what you said.'

The young man put his hand on the priest's shoulder.

'I am going out to speak to the soldiers,' he said. 'I will tell them that I want to fetch food for the people here – all of the people here.'

'But you cant… '

'Yes, I can. Just tell everyone that that is what I am going to do.'

He went to the church door. The gunmen seized their weapons and leapt to their feet in one movement. In a second they surrounded the stranger, their guns trained on him. Simultaneously Father Marcus intervened, forced his way between stranger and gunmen.

'Let him go!' shouted the priest, trembling with fear. 'He is going for food. Let him go, I say!'

No one moved. Father Marcus, trembling almost uncontrollably, eyed each of the gunmen in turn. Slowly they lowered their Kalashnikovs.

The stranger quietly opened the church door, buttoned his anorak, and walked out into the cloud-heavy morning light.

There were a dozen or more soldiers on the village street. They raised their guns. Four of them gathered swiftly behind him to prevent his return to the church.

'I am unarmed,' said the stranger simply, to them all. 'I am going to find food for those in the church. Please let me pass.'

There was silence in the square. No one moved.

'Now!' barked the officer.

A shot was fired. The stranger sank to the ground, spilling blood.

Father Marcus heard the shot. He strode at once to the base of the bell tower. He ignored the gunmen. He grabbed the bell rope, and he pulled and pulled and pulled. The single bell swung irregularly. Father

Marcus was not sure whether he was sounding a cry for help, tolling a death, or celebrating a victory. He only knew he had to ring and ring and ring.

And the sound of the bell floated over the village, rising until it died away on the clouded hills above.

At last Father Marcus could ring no more. He sank onto a chair. Mayor, villagers and gunmen gathered round him, looked down at him. The gunmen said nothing. The mayor spoke.

'We'd hoped,' he said, with deep sadness in his voice, 'that he would… he would… '

'I know,' said Father Marcus, 'I know. I know.'

The eyesight test

Early in April 2002, President Bush asked Prime Minister Sharon to withdraw Israeli forces from occupied West Bank towns 'now'. There was no immediate withdrawal but there was a major battle in Jenin. Commenting on the actions of Israeli forces, the EU's aid commissioner said: 'I am deeply concerned about the way in which basic principles of humanitarian law are being flouted.' The White House described Israeli Prime Minister Sharon as 'a man of peace'.

The Boss's wife was standing by the window.

'I really do think you should have your eyes tested, dear,' she said. 'I think you have bumped into another problem – a big one this time. He sounded very angry on the phone. He's on his way back. He'll be here soon.'

'He' was The Owner of the estate. The Owner spent a lot of time travelling, visiting other estates around the country; leaving The Boss effectively in sole charge much of the time. The Boss was not expecting The Owner's sudden return, but he wasn't unduly bothered. Things were, after all, under control, he felt, as he sat on the sofa watching the TV news of his war against evil gangs.

He certainly wasn't going to have his eyes tested. He would not, he felt, look so impressive if he wore glasses. 'And,' he said to himself, 'being in charge of The Great Estate means that it's more important for me to act firmly than to see clearly.'

In any case, he was sure he could see quite clearly what he needed to see. When the evil gang suicidally attacked The Great Estate and killed many innocent tenants, he had immediately seen the gross injustice of that. And he had acted firmly. He had at once declared war on the evil gang, on all evil gangs everywhere. He had sent his soldiers into the distant estate that was home to this particular evil gang. And the war was going well, as the TV showed. His soldiers were progressively destroying the gang and its supporters.

His wife joined him on the sofa. She watched the news too. And she noticed that the soldiers, as they made their way through the estate, destroying the evil gang, were also killing many innocent people. She pointed this out to her husband. But The Boss didn't see this as unjust, as it was happening a long way away.

His wife got up and turned off the TV.

'He sounded very angry,' she repeated. 'It's about that other war, isn't it – the nasty little war? She explored his face with her eyes, as if looking for bruises. 'Are you sure you haven't bumped into a problem?'

'I haven't bumped into it,' said The Boss. 'I've seen it very clearly all along. And it isn't another war. It's the same war.'

He was of course referring to the conflict going on in a small estate at the other end of the country; where a suicidal gang was killing innocent people. He'd seen it all on TV. This gang was just like the gang that had attacked The Great Estate. It was therefore his enemy. The manager of the small estate, who was using his strong army to try to destroy the gang, was therefore his ally, helping him in his great war against evil gangs. The Boss saw this perfectly clearly from afar.

But the travelling Owner of The Great Estate saw things differently. And he happened to be on the spot. He had had a special affection for the small estate since childhood and was concerned about its troubles. He had decided to visit it. What he saw shocked and saddened him. He was deeply disturbed by the violence of suicidal gang and army alike. He understood the desperation and despair on the one side, the chronic insecurity on the other. He was moved by the sufferings of innocent people on both sides. And he was disturbed by the lack of any real commitment to peacemaking by leaders on either. He was especially angry when, after a particularly bloody battle, soldiers prevented him from going to help their wounded victims.

Then, in a state of distress over this ancient land, which he loved, he heard the news from his own estate. The Boss had just announced to the whole country that he could see very clearly from far away that the manager of the small estate with his violent army was 'a man of peace'.

The Owner was furious. He phoned The Boss. The Boss was out. His wife took the call. The Owner said he would be back the next morning and wished to see The Boss at once. And from the tone of The Owner's voice, she rightly sensed that her husband had bumped into a big problem.

The Owner burst into the room without knocking. He told The Boss in no uncertain terms that, if he wished to continue to manage The Great Estate, he must have his eyes tested at once. The Boss's wife said: 'That's what I have been telling him for months.'

The next day, The Owner himself drove the Boss, with his wife, to an eye specialist. The Owner waited outside in the car. The Boss went in with his wife.

The specialist, after careful tests, did indeed discover a serious defect.

He told The Boss: 'I'm afraid your eyes cannot see injustice properly. You see it clearly on your own doorstep, but not on the other side of the world. You see it when you are the victim, but not when you are the cause. You see its symptoms, but not its causes. And I think you have spent too much time looking at television pictures of your war against evil gangs, so that destroying them is now the only kind of justice you recognize.'

The wife of The Boss asked the specialist what the remedy was.

The specialist said: 'Your husband will have to wear thick glasses for the rest of his life.'

When the wife of The Boss told The Owner, he was not surprised. In his travels he had come across many people whose eyesight seemed to him to be lacking in the same way – not least the people on both sides in the war-torn, troubled estate he loved so much.

And as he drove The Boss and his wife home, he told them a story from long ago, about a man who was once told by a very famous specialist that he should remove the plank from his own eye so that he could see clearly to remove a speck from his brother's.

Underneath the weeping willow tree

On June 20th 2002 Palestinian gunmen killed three children in a raid on an Israeli settlement. The following night Israeli soldiers killed three children in an incursion into Jenin. Sadly these are just two of many entries in the catalogue of children killed in the global war waged by and against terrorists.

It was a warm spring day. The sun shone gently down on the grassy hillside above the city. Clusters of wild flowers, celebrating the spring, had distributed themselves over the grass. Children too had distributed themselves – the older ones sitting or strolling, some in groups, some alone, the younger ones playing spasmodically. A little boy of four and an older girl, who had decided to mother him, picked forget-me-nots together.

A mile away, the city ground on at its daily work. Cars and trucks made their way round the ring road below the hill, sounded their horns, queued at the lights, then grumbled off again in low gear.

The children were aware of none of this. Their only world now was the hillside, bounded by a fence at the bottom, and at the top by tall pines, standing shoulder to shoulder, like sentinels guarding the summit of the hill.

The pines seemed unconcerned about the children. But below them, alone in a damp depression on the hillside, stood another tree, a weeping willow, its slender trailing branches clothed in spring green, reaching down toward the ground, its trunk leaning towards the children, feeling for them, sharing their underlying distress.

In was a Saturday afternoon. A woman, with her head down, walked slowly along the path by the fence at the bottom of the hill, then began to follow its winding way up the hillside towards the children. She carried a bunch of flowers she'd bought from the shop in town. She paused to gain breath. She looked up but she could not see the children, for they were dead.

She saw only what the dead children could not see – their own memorials: rows of graves, each a marble rectangle set in mown grass, surrounded by a tidy path, every grave the same size and at the lower end of each a simple inscription – the child's name, dates of birth and death and above the inscription a photograph framed in marble, a snapshot of a living face frozen onto the grave.

The woman knelt by her little boy's grave: 'Joshua 1998–2002'. She looked at his picture and she wept as she removed last week's flowers and arranged the fresh bunch she had brought.

Unseen by her, the children watched her, as they watched every grieving parent who came to this memorial park, as the living called it. From a little further up the hill, near the willow, Joshua recognized his mother. He ran, half tumbling down the slope, forget-me-nots in hand, to his own grave. He called 'Mummy!' He tried to hug her, longed for her to pick him up. But she heard nothing, felt no touch, sensing not his presence but his absence.

She remembered the horror of the day he died. After a night of terrifying shelling, she had gone out in the clear dawn with him to find food. She remembered the whine of the late shell shattering the stillness, the explosion which blew her off her feet, and then finding Joshua's little body beneath the rubble.

Heavily she stood and began to walk among the other graves, every one of them a memorial to a child killed in war. Trying to comfort herself she said: 'He is at peace now. They are all at peace.'

But she was wrong. They were none of them at peace. Her son had died too young to understand why not. But the older children knew. They knew the terrible truth they had found on dying, which they carried with them every day on the hillside. They knew that there could be no peace for dead children until living grown-ups stopped killing living children in war.

In the land of the living, they say that a burden shared is a burden halved. But in the land of the dead, the reverse is true. The more innocent children killed in war, the greater the burden on the dead becomes – the burden of an accumulating truth: that the living are giving the dead no peace.

And the dead children knew no way to relieve themselves of the burden by sending a message back to the living. Every day living parents and grandparents, brothers and sisters would come to the hillside, bringing flowers, to grieve. Dignitaries would come on special occasions. Every day the living remembered the dead with genuine sadness. And the willow wept with them all. But the children had no way to communicate to the visitors the message they so urgently needed to share.

Every day the dead longed to touch the living, to speak, to shout. 'Stop! Tell them to stop, to stop killing children!' But no word could be heard.

'If only,' the older ones said to each other, 'if only we could return from the dead and hold up signs, like school crossing wardens, saying "Stop! Let the children pass through life in safety."' But they knew of no way back.

The afternoon passed. Joshua's mother went, and Joshua continued to play with the older girl, picking forget-me-nots. Other parents came and went – and a small group of foreign visitors, who stood sadly for a while, but who had no particular grave on which to focus their sadness.

Evening came. The sun, hazy now, was setting over the city, tingeing the weeping willow with gold. Under the willow sat a man. The children had not noticed him come. And he showed no sign of going. The children kept looking at him and he kept watching them. Slowly the children realized that he was one of them. He was not living. He was dead. And he was crying, crying on the hillside above the city. And none of the children felt they should approach him – none that is except little Joshua.

Joshua edged nearer the willow. Protectively the girl followed close behind. The man wiped his eyes and beckoned to them, smiling.

'Come to me,' they heard him say.

He held out his arms to Joshua and Joshua trotted forward. The man took him on his knee and Joshua gave him his bunch of forget-me-nots. They drooped now, for wild flowers soon wilt when picked.

'Go and bring the others,' said the man gently, encouragingly, to the girl. And she did.

All the children stood silently round him

'What did you want to say?' he asked, with an inviting smile.

They told him why there was no peace for dead children. He listened but it was as though he were listening to something he already knew. They said they so much needed to get their message back to the living. He understood that at once. It was as though the very reason for which he had come was to be their messenger.

'But how?' they wanted to know, eagerly;. 'How can you take back our message?'

'You will see tomorrow,' he said. 'Or rather,' he added with a smile, 'you will not see!'

And with that they had to be content. None of them dared ask the man any more questions. They thanked him, said goodnight and walked away, leaving him alone.

Joshua took the older girl's hand.

'Will the man tell Mummy that I love her?' he asked.

'I'm sure he will,' said the girl. 'But she knows that already.'

By morning the man was gone. The children half expected him to return the next evening to tell them what he had done, that he had delivered their message. They hardly dared to hope that the living would listen, that the killing of children would stop, that they would find peace.

The man never returned. The children remain disturbed, without peace, and more dead children join them every day. But they have not given up hope, for, although he was with them for such a short while, they believe they can trust the man who came to visit them that Saturday evening.

Joshua's mother still comes each week to tend his grave. And the willow tree weeps still.

The forgotten lamp

Early in May 2002, Prime Minister Sharon of Israel flew to Washington to see President Bush. Sharon said: 'He who rises up to kill us, we will pre-empt it, and kill him first.' The President acknowledged Israel's right to self-defence, but added the hope that the Prime Minister would do something about the plight of the Palestinian people, 'in accordance with Israel's own values'.

Peter picked his way through the rubble of what had been his house, his family home. It was the first time he had been back since the shell hit it, since the funeral of his little daughter, killed outright as the blast brought the wall down on top of her.

He had left his wife, Rachel, in his brother Samuel's house, now their temporary home. She had hardly spoken since the attack. She would not be comforted. Most of the time she lay on the bed, with her face to the wall, repeating ancestral laments – "Is there any sorrow like my sorrow?"… "My God, why have you forsaken me?" And village women visiting her wept too, shedding tears for a whole people whose ancient sufferings were being recycled.

The enemy attacks had become more frequent in recent months. The mountainside village was now very vulnerable in disputed territory. Rachel had argued with her husband that they should move out. But Peter would not leave. The village was fortified, soldiers patrolled it day and night. To move, he felt deep down, would be to opt out of his people's story, a long story in which life and land, sacrifice and survival had always been interwoven. Peter would not desert his village. And Rachel would not leave Peter.

Now the bereaved father searched among the rubble for things belonging to his daughter which might comfort his wife a little. He clambered around the crumbled wall, carefully dragging broken roof timbers aside. He studied the crater made by the shell, and he noticed a hole in one side of it. The shell seemed to have exposed a cave in the rock that had supported the wall of the house. Peter began to scrape rubble from the entrance to the cave. He made an opening wide enough to crawl through. But inside it was dark and unknown, possibly dangerous. He turned his back on the hole. He resumed his search for his little girl's things, found a doll and a jacket and then walked back to his brother's house.

For the rest of the day he forgot the cave. But that night it came to haunt him, to invite him. He imagined himself entering the hole, lying still in the crypt of his life, looking for refuge from present pain in the darkness of the past.

The next morning, early, he returned to his house with a torch. He lowered himself into the crater and, with the torch, peered into the cave. He crawled in carefully, aware of the risk of rock fall. The cave had no definable shape that Peter could see. Its walls and roof were rough jagged rock. It was big enough to sit in. The floor was uneven but smooth, suggesting that someone might have levelled it at some time long ago. There was a small pile of loose rocks on the floor.

He was attracted by the rock on top of the pile. It seemed more regular in shape than the others. Peter crawled towards it. He picked it up. It was light. It was not rock. It was smooth. It was thin metal, oval in shape, with a curved handle at one end and a narrowing lip at the other. It was an old oil lamp.

Peter brought the lamp up to the daylight. He dusted it with his hand. The metal was dull and grey, but the lamp was undamaged. He took it to his brother's house and gently began to clean it. Samuel showed little interest in the lamp, but was glad that his brother had found some occupation to distract him from his grief.

Peter became increasingly fascinated, as, with his careful polishing, the silver began to shine, and the beautiful ornamentation of handle and rim revealed itself. At last he set the lamp on the table, found a wick and filled the lamp with oil. As dusk gathered, he took it to the bedroom and lit it. Rachel lay with her face to the wall. Peter sat on the edge of the bed and watched the flame gather strength. He wondered how long it was since anyone else had seen the light of this strange lamp.

He could not recall how long he sat and watched. He became

entranced. He vaguely remembered Rachel, sitting beside him for a while, watching the flame with him. Then she lay down again. But Peter continued to study the flame, feeling himself drawn into it as though down an endless fiery tunnel. He thought he saw things long buried in the past, things he had never imagined before, burning brightly before him.

He was disturbed and excited by what he saw, and slept little. The next morning he tried, inadequately he felt, to explain to Rachel and Samuel. His mind dragged disjointed phrases out of his mouth.

'I looked into the flame and saw… a vision… of our nation as it was meant to be… long ago.'

'The golden age,' said Samuel, capturing Peter's half formed thoughts in a hackneyed phrase.

'I don't mean that,' said Peter. 'I mean… it was as though… as though something was decided about us long ago, and then buried, like the lamp, for a long time. And… and it's taken that shell, and the death of… to… to bring it to light. That lamp is saying something about us, to us, about… our destiny as a nation?'

Conscious of his own uncertainty, he looked to Rachel for encouragement but she did not look at him. Peter felt alone.

Samuel was suddenly impatient.

'What destiny? We're in the middle of a war, for heaven's sake. You have lost your daughter, your home. Rachel's grief stricken. Our destiny's in our hands, our guns.'

'We were meant for something better. We're walking in darkness. We need… a light.'

Samuel did not understand. He shrugged his shoulders and left the room. Rachel understood – or she thought she did. She took Peter's hand and looked him sorrowfully in the face. Unlike her, she thought, he could not face the finality of their loss. She knew there was no escape from it. There was nothing but a blank wall now. But he, poor man, was seeking distraction in polishing an old lamp, refuge in a world of his own imagining.

Samuel walked up and down in the yard. He too dismissed the lamp talk. He was sorry for his brother, whose grief was undermining his common sense. He felt he must help Peter to harness grief to anger and anger to retaliation. The only reality that mattered, he thought, was defending the village, driving back the enemy.

But Peter would not set the lamp aside. He continued to polish it during the day, and as light faded again he lit it, this time on the living room table. Peter watched. Rachel sat with him. Samuel, uneasy, like an animal sensing earthquake, paced the room for a while; then he went outside and tried to busy himself in the yard.

The shell landed, at the other end of the street. The blast blew open the door, blew over the lamp. The oil spilled, the flame spread across the table. Rachel screamed. Peter did not move; he was fascinated by the spreading flame. It was to him not just a consequence of the explosion, but a response to it. But Samuel, rushing in, saw only a fire in the making, grabbed a rug, extinguished the flames – and then tuned on his brother.

'Get that damned thing out of my house!' he shouted. 'Put it back where it came from! Do you hear me?'

And before he went to bed, Peter did take the lamp back to his own house. He hid it under the rubble, where he would easily find it in the morning.

Rachel also wanted the lamp out of the way and before they went to sleep she persuaded Peter to take it to the museum in the nearby city. She hoped that a prosaic explanation might extinguish his obsession with the lamp, might free him to share with her the reality of their unmitigated loss and grief.

The next day, inside the museum, Jacob the scholarly old curator stood by the window of his study. He was more than interested. He was excited. Bright sunlight shone on his face, and on the silver lamp in his hand. Peter sat at a table shaded from the sun by ceiling-high bookshelves. He watched the old man as he slowly turned the lamp round and over, round and over again in his hands. Peter read the excitement on his face, but resisted the impulse to question him. Peter waited.

Jacob returned from the window, placed the lamp reverently on the table. From the bookshelves, scarcely searching, he took the book he wanted, and turned almost at once to the right page.

'Here it is, you see. Here it is – the story of the lamp! Listen!"

Jacob began to read, quickly, stumbling over the words.

It was an old tale about a prophet who climbed a mountain to ask God why he allowed never-ending conflict between his people and their neighbours. God at first apparently had nothing to say. Then there was a thunderstorm. The prophet sheltered in a cave. Lightning struck a rock in front of the cave. The rock blazed with a fierce tall flame.

'The storm passed,' Jacob went on, not reading, but telling the story quickly in his own words. 'The prophet saw that lightning had split the rock open and in the cleft a small flame still burned. It came from a silver lamp, wedged in the rock.'

'You mean… a lamp like this?' asked Peter, pointing

'That is the lamp!' shouted Jacob triumphantly. He slammed the book shut and dropped it on the table. The lamp jumped. Jacob's eyes were bright. He had found a long lost treasure. He was emphatic. 'God left his answer in the lamp!'

The old curator raised the lamp from the table and held it in front of Peter, his hands shaking a little.

'The prophet lifted the lamp from the rock. He had the answer in his hands!'

'What answer?'

'This lamp, Peter, is The Light of the Nations! It's the lamp of peace. God chose his people to bring peace to their neighbours. And only in their peace will we find ours. Do you understand? The prophet took the burning lamp down the mountain, showed it to the war-torn people. He left it for posterity – for us to find!

The old man paused, put a quivering hand on Peter's shoulder, then went on. 'And you, my good and truly fortunate friend, have rediscovered this lamp among the ruin and suffering of our war.'

Exhausted by his own emotion, Jacob replaced the lamp on the table and sat down beside Peter.

Peter, feeling he had just received a blessing, asked: 'And is that all?'

'No, that is not all. Tradition says that whoever finds the lamp must rekindle the flame, recall people to its light.'

'You mean… you mean,' asked Peter, 'that I must become a sort of… sort of prophet of the lamp?'

Jacob nodded. Peter thought of Rachel, waiting for him to return to their mountain village, to tell her that the lamp was safely stored away in a museum cupboard.

Jacob read the hesitation in Peter's face but persisted. 'The ancient promise is this: that the ruler who receives this lamp and keeps the flame burning will be the one to bring peace at last to this and every nation. You must take The Light of the Nations to the President. '

'Me? Me take it to the President? The President's hardly likely… '

'I will come with you,' said the curator quietly. 'I will arrange things.'

'But what do I say?' persisted Peter.

Jacob ignored the question. 'Come on,' he said, 'we need oil for the lamp.'

They were not able to see the President. The old curator, in his enthusiasm, had overestimated the influence of his cousin who worked in the presidential offices. And the President was in any case preoccupied with his army chief, planning retaliation against a sequence of enemy attacks on mountain villages. They were, however, able to see the President's press officer.

Peter placed the lamp on the press officer's desk and Jacob retold its story. The press officer listened impatiently, for he had quickly grasped the value of the lamp.

He was a small man, made to look smaller by his big desk, on which his laptop sat open, so that his face was half hidden behind its raised screen. He beamed at his visitors then began typing furiously, his fingers dancing on the keyboard. He talked quickly at the same time. He did not recall ever having heard of the Light of the Nations before, but his imagination pole-vaulted over his ignorance, and raced ahead.

'The timing's brilliant; the location spot on. Here's the story,' he said. 'The enemy – ruthless vandals, iconoclasts – try to destroy our national heritage, our most sacred site. And this brave man… Excuse me, what did you say your name was?'

'Peter,' said Peter. 'But it wasn't like… '

'This one brave man, ennobled by his grief, risks his life to save our nation's treasured possession for posterity.'

He looked up, and stopped typing, peered over his laptop, smiling. 'I'll insert a suitable quote from the President – something like,' he paused, '… something like… ' And he began tapping at the keyboard again.

'Excuse me!' said Peter, firmly. 'Excuse me!' He was surprised by his own boldness.

The press officer was surprised too – surprised to be interrupted. He looked over his laptop again.

'Yes?'

'I would like to light the lamp.'

'Light the lamp?' said the press officer, 'Why?'

'I will tell you,' said Peter. And he lit the lamp.

The press officer watched the flame for a moment or two. His face hardened. Then he bent over his laptop again, and continued to compose suitable words for the President. His fingers worked the keyboard more slowly, more deliberately, now. Peter waited for him to look up. He did not, so Peter spoke to the top of the press officer's head.

'It is not the enemy that wants to destroy the lamp. It is we who have forgotten where we left it. Before ever the enemy brought my house down, we had buried the lamp. The story people need to hear is not how I found the lamp, but how the prophet found it, and what it has to say to us.'

Jacob nodded.

'I have the book,' he said and stood, offering it to the press officer.

The press officer ignored the book. Carefully he put his laptop on standby, and closed down the screen. There was silence.

The press officer stared at Peter from the other side of the burning lamp. His smile had faded now.

'We are fighting a war,' he said coldly, 'against an enemy determined to destroy our nation. There can be no compromise with such an enemy. It is a war we must win. And we will win it if we are united in our resolve to do so. I must warn you… er, in fairness I think I should warn you, that comments which may lead some of our people to question the justice of our cause, could weaken that resolve. Such comments would… er… not be welcome.'

The press officer stood.

'You must excuse me now,' he said. He bent forward, blew out the lamp and picked it up.

'I think it best if I keep this,' he added officiously, and moved to put it in a cupboard.

'No!' shouted Peter. 'No!' Quickly he moved round the desk and seized the lamp. The press officer stood speechless as Peter carried it out of the room, with Jacob following.

In bed that night, Peter told Rachel the whole story of the day. Rachel was glad that he had left the lamp at the museum, for the curator to look after.

Peter knew that the story of the lamp was not over, that soon he must recover it, relight it, retell its message. Rachel sensed that too but she had her husband back now, and that night she slept in peace in his arms, for the first time since their child was killed.

Peter's brother Samuel had forgotten the lamp already. More troops had moved into the village during the day. The army was preparing to regain lost ground.

Descantia's new song

There was a public meeting in New York in May 2002, held to discuss plans to build again on the site of the fallen World Trade Center. One speaker asked the city officials: 'Please give us a skyline that will once again cause our spirits to soar.'

Descantia took the day off.

For months, the government had been warning people that the next attack was a matter not of 'if' but of 'when'. And the city's mayor had repeated the message often enough.

Now 'when' had happened. The hotel where Descantia were due to perform had been wrecked by a suicide bomber the previous evening. There would be no guests for them to sing to in the riverside restaurant, for there was now no restaurant.

So the group had no need to rehearse that day, and nothing else to do. The morning sun shone bright out of a cloudless sky. It would be a hot day. So the four of them, two men and two women, piled into a car and set off for the coast.

Their journey started slowly. Checkpoints, quickly set up during the night, added to the usual road congestion. Police stopped Descantia, studied their faces, inspected their car. Traffic crawled along the main road through the downtown area. One side of the road was lined with shabby shops and houses, many boarded up, and workless men stood smoking at street corners, beneath advertisements for cars they would never be able to buy. On the other side flowed the river, its banks marked with disused and crumbling jetties and stunted grey trees, whose lower branches had managed to hook passing plastic bags that trailed in the water.

Clear at last of the city, Descantia stopped for morning coffee at a riverside bar. They chose a table outside by the water. The city skyline was just visible on the horizon, shimmering indistinctly in the heat.

Descantia were glad of a day out of it. They needed to decide about the future. Audiences had been falling for some while, ever since terrorists destroyed the great tower. A new sense of insecurity walked the wealthy streets. People were leery of public gatherings now. There were more empty tables in the posh restaurant where Descantia sang, fewer Rolex watches and less wrist jewellery on display as guests toyed with after-dinner brandies. Obsequious waiters were less rushed. And applause for the group's songs was polite now rather than enthusiastic. Audiences used to enjoy their ironic descants upon the confident melodies of city life. They laughed at themselves in Descantia's musical mirror. But an establishment that can laugh at itself when it feels secure loses its sense of humour when a bomb unexpectedly falls on its principal security symbol, kills a lot of people, and spreads a lot of grief. There seemed no place for irony now. Self-criticism, however witty and melodious, seemed off key, verging on the unpatriotic.

Descantia felt like prophets rejected by their people and not particularly thankful for the gift of music they had been given. 'Should we,' they asked themselves over several cups of riverside coffee, 'sing a different kind of song, reassuring, patriotic for a city, a nation, at war? Or should we just break up?'

Suddenly they put their thoughts on hold. For on the water in front of them had landed a flock of beautiful birds. They could not name, had never seen, such birds. The birds looked out of place. Perhaps they had lost their way, were migrants off course, visitors from another world. These strange creatures steadily rode the water, their heads pointing upstream towards the city skyline. They seemed to be watching Descantia. Descantia watched the birds too, for some while, in silence. Then, as one, without a word, almost reverently, the singers stood up, left their coffee, and walked to the very edge of the river. They continued to watch, as the current steered the birds closer and closer to the bank.

Back in the city, the day had begun early for the Mayor. He had visited the shattered restaurant in the small hours, then the hospital, trying to comfort the grieving. Dawn broke. He went to his office and sat, wondering whether to cancel the meeting he had prearranged for that day. He decided not to. 'Definitely not!' he said to the city architect who phoned early to enquire. Then he summoned his press officer. Together they prepared a statement.

'Speaking early this morning, amid the wreckage of the restaurant, the Mayor said… '

And now, the Mayor stood with his back to the window of his conference room, waiting for members of his management team to arrive. Automatically he noted the arrangements. Mineral water and glasses, note pads and ballpoints with the city logo were all properly arranged on the veneered conference table. The air conditioning was on, ready to protect the city's managers against the heat of the coming day.

The Mayor turned to the window. He looked down on the river which ran through the city centre, shielded from the traffic by parallel rows of healthy trees on either bank. He looked up at skyline. He had not got used to it. He felt he never would. Ever since the attack destroyed the tower, the skyline seemed to stare at him like a handsome face marred by a missing tooth, most evident when the city smiled at itself in the mirror, by the light of the morning sun. Admittedly the gap in the skyline let more light into his conference room. That was useful. Nonetheless, he resented the disfigurement of the city. He as mayor must repair it. It was his duty. It was his mission.

The meeting assembled. First came the architect, with plans to present, then the heads of finance, public works and, of course, security. They all sat down, placing their mobile phones on the table by their notepads.

The head of security made a brief report on the bombing of the restaurant, on heightened security, police checkpoints and such like. The Mayor then read from his press statement.

'We are at war… government warnings have, sadly, been fully justified… my deepest sympathy goes out to… be assured, we will root out this evil of terrorism… security is our paramount concern… And we will build a new tower, greater, stronger than the first… last night's attack is no reason to delay; on the contrary… Plans will be made public this evening. The tower will not celebrate a victory. Its conception, its creation will itself be a victory for civilization over the axis of evil.'

All agreed with these decisive and inspirational sentiments – all, that is, except the spirits in the room. And as the architect prepared his presentation, and the others sipped their mineral water in anticipation, the spirits rose to go. Unseen and unheard they had come in. Unseen and unheard they now went out – sad, anxious and agitated. They knew they had little time left.

They had come to the meeting after months of increasingly weary roaming around the city. They had come hoping that the city leaders would pause, would allow them time to make their presentation, to place their message gently on the table among the water glasses, notepads and mobiles. They hoped the living would at last listen. Then they, the spirits, would be able to put their burden down and soar heavenward as the spirits of the dead should.

These spirits had lived embodied lives in the high tower. It had been their home. It was, they thought, the pinnacle of human achievement, radiating the message of security through prosperity to the city, the nation, the world. They thought themselves privileged to dwell on the skyline where earth and heaven meet.

When evil brought the tower down, the spirits found themselves suddenly disembodied, homeless. At first they stayed close to the grieving to comfort them, to the brave to inspire them. Then they began to wander. They roamed among the elite in posh restaurants, like unseen waiters between the tables. They drifted in the dawn mist on the tidy ornamented river in the city centre. Then they floated downstream with the flotsam and discovered the river's collection of plastic bags. They explored the downtown and hovered in the cigarette smoke over the kitchen tables of the poor and powerless.

They felt the truth of what they saw in a way that tower-bound living folk do not, and the more they saw, the more burdened they felt. They became weary. They searched with increasing urgency for someone on whom they could download their message, so that they could move on. But they found no one. They found the city too busy licking recent wounds to heal old ones, smouldering too much with righteous anger against those who had brought down its tower.

The Mayor's meeting finally entombed their dwindling hopes. The city leaders, it seemed to the spirits, were more concerned with trying to stamp out the new-found insecurity of the powerful than with healing the longstanding insecurity of the powerless. The meeting wanted to reaffirm the old order, rather than create a new one.

And what these burdened spirits so much wanted to tell the Mayor and his team was that the city needed not a new tower but a new skyline, not new building from below, but new light from above, space to allow the city from above to engage with the city below; a more open and porous border between heaven and earth.

The falling of the old tower had let new light into the conference room, onto plans for a new tower that would cut out the light and darken the conference room again. The spirits smiled sadly at this irony. They left the Mayor's meeting like failed angels, like weary birds with no place to land, and too tired to fly. They felt that, by the end of the afternoon, the door on a new future would be closed.

It was time for them to leave the city for ever. Wearily, their wings almost touching the water, they flew slowly down river, to the sea. But the sea proved too far for them to fly. So they landed by the riverside bar, and turned to take one last distant look at the skyline. They had just enough strength to paddle against the current and hold their position, but not for much longer. Soon they would turn and allow the river to carry them down to into infinite waters. Then they saw Descantia.

Birds and singers were very, very close now, almost touching. The birds gazed at the skyline now. Descantia gazed at the birds.

Then, suddenly, Descantia reached out and caught the message. Fragments of lyric, snatches of melody – together they caught them and held them firmly.

'Give us a skyline… to make our spirits soar… '

At once the birds began to tremble, to flutter in anticipation. Then, as one, they rose gracefully from the water and flew up river, back towards the city, gaining height, gaining strength.

Descantia followed below, earth bound, in the car, stopping and starting in the traffic. They sang, trying out words and music, composing as they drove. The police were still checking cars. Descantia sang at the checkpoints. The police sensed no danger in the song, did not recognize it as subversive.

> Please give us a skyline.
> To make our spirits soar again.
> Listen to our song sign
> Which points to heaven again.

Imagination's taught us
That the river is our soul.
God singing on its waters
Will make our city whole.

So please listen to our song sign
Of hope to heal the pain.
Open up the skyline
And let our spirits soar again.

This was far from polished. Descantia knew that. But this was not an after-dinner song for a posh restaurant. It was a song for the streets, a song for the skyline. And it was a song for this evening. Descantia felt they must hurry. They did not know why. But the birds above them knew why. The Mayor would soon bring his meeting to a close. The announcement about the new tower was imminent.

The Mayor's meeting had in fact dragged on. The early evening sun was streaming through the conference room window. And the air conditioning had for some reason failed. The room was no longer a cool executive cocoon. It was a hot house.

The discussion flagged. The Mayor got up to open the window. The sound of singing floated up from the street below. A small crowd had gathered around a group of singers, under a tree by the riverside. The words were indistinct above the traffic noise, but fragments of melody floated upwards.

The Mayor stared out of the window. He was only vaguely conscious of the singing, and of the setting sunlight streaking the river with gold. His concern was how to conclude the meeting, how to formulate the decisive question.

Then something caught his eye. A flock of birds rose from the river, up and up they flew, through the gap in the skyline left by the fallen tower. The Mayor watched, till he could see no more as the birds were consumed in the blazing sunset.

But the birds had left him with a distracting thought. He said to himself: 'I will never see a sunset like this from my window if we build high again.'

He returned to his seat at the head of the table and glanced at his watch.

'Well,' he said, 'we have talked enough. We've studied the plans, studied the figures. I've promised an announcement for the news deadline. We mustn't appear indecisive, not after what happened last night. It's decision time.'

He paused. He looked out of the window and, still looking out of the window, he said, slowly: 'Should we build a tower or leave the space open to the sky?'

His colleagues stared at him, in astonishment. It was not the question they were expecting. It was not the question he had meant to ask.

The meeting stayed silent, trying to catch the song as it floated through the open window.

Bible references

1 A letter to the President – *Jeremiah 5:28; 8:15; 9:21; 20:9; 22:3; 25:32; 36*

2 Wanted dead or alive – *1 Samuel 25*

3 Conversation in the cockpit – *Exodus 16; Mark 6:30-44*

4 God bless America – *The book of Job*

5 Marjon's last journey – *Isaiah 11:6-9; Luke 2:8-16*

6 Draining the swamp – *Genesis 6:11 – 9:17*

7 My dream interview – *Matthew 27:24; Mark 8:27; 13:2; 14:32-43, 56-59; John 2:19; 8:25, 32, 58; 11:48-50; 18:37,38*

8 In the cool of the evening – *Genesis 3*

9 The moment of truth – *Judges 16; Psalm 72:1-4; Acts 9:1-9*

10 The four wise men – *Matthew 2:1-18*

11 Execution on video – *Acts 22:1-11; 23:12-22; Ephesians 2*

12 The axis of evil – *Exodus 4:10-17; 32:1-24*

13 Slaying the dragon – *Luke 4:5-8; 14:31; 22:24-27*

14 Amos and daughter – *Amos esp. 5:24; 7:14*

15 The Passover massacre – *Exodus 11–14*

16 Father Marcus rings the bell – *Luke 24:13-21*

17 The eyesight test – *Matthew 7:1-4*

18 Underneath the weeping willow tree – *Mark 10:14*

19 The forgotten lamp – *Isaiah 9:2-6; 49:6; Lamentations 1:12; Psalm 22:1*

20 Descantia's new song – *Genesis 11:1-9; Revelation 21:1-4; 22:1-4*